Every Day above a New Horizon

The story of a journey

John Davison

Every Day above a New Horizon

By John Davison

ISBN: 9781493505586

Copyright © 2013 John Davison

The right of John Davison to be identified as the author of this work has been asserted by him in accordance with the Copyright, Designs and Patents Act, 1988.

This book is sold subject to the conditions that it shall not, by way of trade or otherwise, be lent, resold, hired out, or otherwise circulated without the author's prior consent in any form of binding or cover other than that in which it is produced and without a similar condition including this condition being imposed on the subsequent purchaser.

Cover pictures © 2013 John Davison.

To Ray Roberts, with thanks.

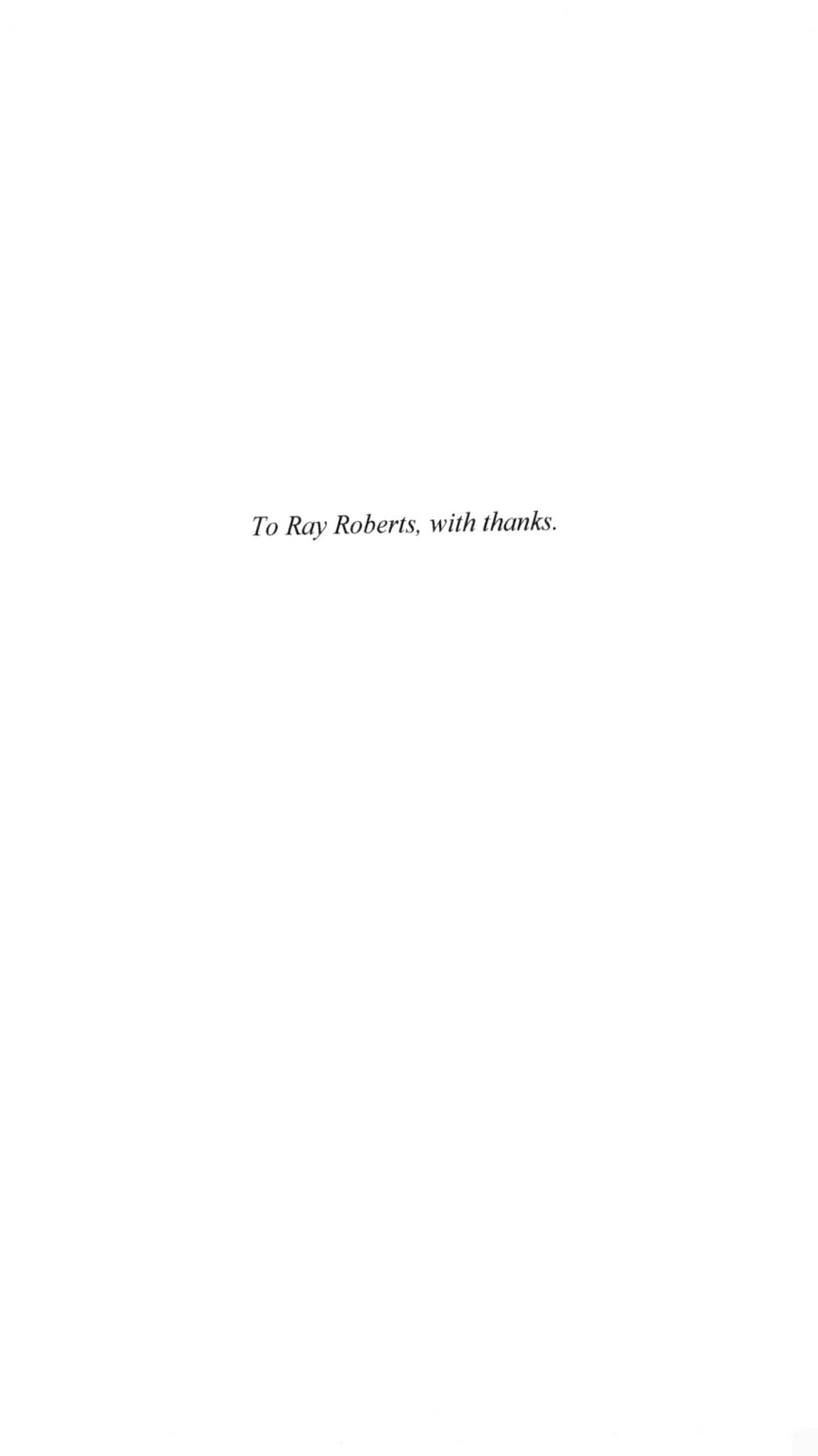

Every Day above a New Horizon

The story of a journey

John Davison

Every Day above a New Horizon

Contents

Introduction: Le Puy-en-Velay

Part 1 – The Route to France

Chapter 1 - Stanage Edge, Derbyshire

Chapter 2 - Dartmoor

Chapter 3 - Cherill Down, Wiltshire

Chapter 4 - The West Highland Way

Chapter 5 - The West Highland Way, Part 2

Chapter 6 - The Great Glen Way

Chapter 7 - The East Highland Way

Part 2 – In the Footsteps of Stevenson

Chapter 8 - Le Puy-en-Velay

Chapter 9 - Langogne

Chapter 10 - Mirandol and Mont Lozere

Chapter 11 - Le Pont-de-Montvert

Chapter 12 - The Cévennes

Every Day above a New Horizon

Introduction
Le Puy-en-Velay

"Everywhere is walking distance if you have the time."
Steven Wright

I stepped off the train onto the platform and pulled on my rucksack. Other passengers bustled past me, but I was able to take the time to smell the air and do up my jacket against the gathering rain.

I'd spent the day on the *Train à Grande Vitesse*, the TGV or high-speed train across France. I'd left home early that morning to get to the international platforms at St Pancras Station and now, just eight hours later, here I was in Le Puy at the start of my walk.

The rain had become torrential and I paused in the station entrance and looked up and down the street outside. I could see my hotel opposite, just a short dash away.

I felt a little self-conscious, as if my rucksack and walking clothes set me apart from the rest of the people here and I felt a slight resentment at that. After all Le Puy is a start point for the *Camino de Santiago*, the popular pilgrimage trail that crosses France and Spain, and numerous *Grande Randonees*, the French long-distance walking trails, pass through it. But I couldn't see anyone else who looked like a walker. It seemed the exact opposite of somewhere like, say, the Lake District, where almost everyone dresses like a walker even if they're only popping out for a loaf of bread. I told myself that I wasn't out of place, my thinking was. It was time to forget about other people, time to do what I'd come here for.

I checked for cars and then my first steps took me out of the railway station, onto the street and into the driving rain. Splash through the puddles and I was into the hotel foyer and checking in.

I'd treated myself to the luxury of four walls and a roof for the first night of my expedition and I was conscious that I'd just taken my first few steps on a journey that had been years in the planning. It wasn't that a journey like this takes a long time to plan, just that circumstances had dictated a long time before I could actually do it, and that had left me with a lot of enforced thinking time. Then, finally, one of those rare, significant life changes had gifted me the opportunity and I'd seized it with both hands.

For many years, I'd worked in London. I had a job I loved and great work colleagues. But my job was a demanding one and it took up a significant portion of my life; I was forced to put many plans on hold to facilitate it.

Almost as a form of escapism I had taken to reading about travel, maybe as a substitute for actually doing it, and I'd particularly liked the writing of Robert Louis Stevenson. I'd enjoyed his children's literature when I was younger and as an adult, confined to work and home, I soaked up his travel writing. I was particularly taken with an excerpt from *An Inland Voyage*, written in 1877. In it, the traveller, Stevenson, expresses the frustration felt by one who wished to emulate him but was unable to because of work and home commitments:

> *One person in Maubeuge, however, showed me something more than his outside. That was the driver of the hotel omnibus: a mean enough looking little man, as well as I can remember; but with a spark of something human in his soul. He had heard of our little journey, and came to me at once in envious sympathy. How he longed to travel! he told me. How he longed to be somewhere else, and see the round world before he went into the grave! "Here I am," said he. "I drive to the station. Well. And then I drive back again to the hotel. And so on every day and all the week round. My God, is that life?" I could not say I thought it was--for him. He pressed me to tell him where I had been, and where I hoped to go; and as he listened, I declare the fellow sighed. Might not this have been a brave African traveller, or gone to the Indies after Drake? But it is an evil age for the gypsily inclined among men. He who can sit squarest on a three-legged stool, he it is who has the wealth and glory.*
>
> *I wonder if my friend is still driving the omnibus for the Grand Cerf? Not very likely, I believe; for I think he was on the eve of mutiny when we passed through, and perhaps our passage determined him for good. Better a thousand times that he should be a tramp, and mend pots and pans by the wayside, and sleep under trees, and see the dawn and the sunset every day above a new horizon.*

I printed off those paragraphs and pinned them to my office wall. As I did so, I had no idea that I would pin them on a total of five office walls across London before I would finally get a chance to act on them.

I was in Le Puy-en-Velay because it contained the nearest railway station to a small town called Le Monastier, and Le Monastier was the starting point for a walk that Robert Louis Stevenson completed in 1878.

The year before, while on the canoeing trip that had taken him to the *Hotel Grand Cerf* in Maubeuge, Stevenson had met the love of his life, an American named Fanny Van de Grift Osbourne. Fanny returned to the States, to a troubled marriage and an eventual divorce. Stevenson needed money to pay for the voyage to join her, and he planned to make that money by walking from Le Monastier to St-Jean-du-Gard and selling his account of the journey.

The product, *Travels with a Donkey in the Cévennes,* was published the following year. It was a success and Stevenson was able to sail the Atlantic to Fanny.

Inspired by Stevenson's writing, confined by commitments at work and at home, I began planning to walk the same route through the Cévennes.

The obvious planning involving food, accommodation and route was relatively simple and soon accomplished. However, I was still chafing at my lack of opportunity to complete the walk, so I stretched my wings by completing shorter walks, sometimes with friends, sometimes alone. Moreover, as I did so I gradually refined my kit, my knowledge and my mental attitude.

For me, metaphorically at least, it was a long and winding road that had led to me shaking the rain from my jacket in a hotel in a small French town.

----- x -----

Every Day above a New Horizon

Part 1

The Route to France

Every Day above a New Horizon

Chapter 1
Stanage Edge, Derbyshire

"Me thinks that the moment my legs begin to move, my thoughts begin to flow."

Henry David Thoreau

April was unusually warm as I set off from Hathersage in the Peak District. It was one of those all too rare spring days: beautiful, heady sunshine, almost out of place in what still looks more like a winter landscape, but gratefully received by anyone who has endured the usual dark, wet English winter.

It wasn't long before I turned off the main road at a stile and walked across a field, feeling my spirits lift in inverse proportion to the traffic noise fading behind me, enjoying the short, springy turf as I crossed the sheep pasture towards the stepping-stones over the River Derwent.

The path led across closely cropped, light green grass down to the clear river. The field, the stepping-stones and the river formed such a lovely scene that I stopped for an early lunch just to enjoy it. Moments like that are all too few and we must seize them when we find them. In my experience of hillwalking, you have to invest a lot of time walking in the rain and the fog to get the occasional dividend of beauty.

There were no leaves on the trees yet, just a faint green tinge that closer inspection showed to be buds. I was expecting more seasonal weather and already I found myself wondering if I was over-equipped for this trip. But I was desperate to get outdoors and give my bivvy bag[1] its first outing of the year. Even if I was carrying too much kit, I was where I wanted to be: not at work, not at home, but outdoors, somewhere remarkable, with what little I needed on my back.

I finished lunch and put the few items I'd used away in my pack, along with the small amount of litter I'd just created, and set out again, enjoying the walk, the sunshine and the countryside around me.

I realised from the dry ground that once I had left the river and the reservoirs behind, I might be struggling for water. I have always worked on the basis of a phrase I once read in a walking article, which went something like, "Water is abundant on British hills", and I've rarely been disappointed. However, today I could see that the ground was very dry and the moor higher up looked drier still.

I approached Ladybower Reservoir thinking that I had better find a way to get down to the shore to fill up all my water bottles. But water is heavy. One litre of water weighs one kilogram, and it is surprisingly easy to use it up quickly. My drinking mug contains 500ml, so a cup of tea, soup before dinner and a hot chocolate last thing would necessitate a litre and a half. Add in a litre of water for breakfast (two cups of tea) and half a litre to sip through the next morning as I was walking and,

---

[1] Bivvy bag or bivouac bag: a sleeping bag cover, usually made from a breathable, weatherproof material.

without anywhere to stock up near my intended campsite, I'd need to carry three litres just to get me through to lunchtime tomorrow. Three litres doesn't sound very much but in terms of weight, we're talking about an extra three kilograms on my back.

There is a school of thought that argues that much of what we regard as tiredness from long-distance walking or other activity is, in fact, not fatigue at all but dehydration. On my last few trips I had deliberately made a point of drinking more water than I thought I needed (hence the 500ml cups of tea) and I had felt better for it. Therefore, I didn't want to scrimp on water on this trip, especially since the Met Office were forecasting an April heatwave for this weekend.

I saw a picnic area marked on the map and as I got closer to it, I could see what looked like a toilet block. It was indeed a toilet block and thanks to the munificence of Derbyshire Dales District Council and its taxpayers, I was able to fill my water bottles from a tap. It was probably clean water, and there was certainly no sign to say it wasn't drinkable, but I popped a purifying tablet into each bottle all the same, to secure the serenity of mind that comes from knowing that digestive catastrophe is unlikely.

I followed the road on past the reservoir, feeling the extra weight of water in my pack, not dragging me down but still noticeable, and passed a pub with a car park full of bikers enjoying the beer, the company and the fine weather. A strange hobby, I felt, spending thousands of pounds on flash motor bikes and close-fitting leather suits. Although they might think backpacking across hills and moors was strange. They would be wrong, of course. That thought leads me to think that it's a good thing we don't all like the same pastimes. The hills would be very crowded if we did. Or the motorbike shops would. One or the other.

I was sorely tempted to join them for a swift pint and a packet of crisps, if only for a short while, but the moor was calling me and I answered its call.

The day got hotter as I crossed farmland and turned onto a wide track, the land opening out a little more, dry and brown. Grass, bracken and a few sparse trees, all in their winter state but all basking in hot sunshine under a cloudless blue sky.

I passed a small clump of trees in a sheltered spot with short grass beneath them. I stepped into the shade and took a pull on my water bottle (careful - don't want to use it up too early!) This would make a marvellous bivvy site. I could imagine preparing my evening meal and watching the sun set from here, then wriggling down into my bivvy bag to watch the stars come out. Good bivvy sites are sometimes like busses: you don't see one for ages, particularly when you want one, then lots come by all at once, usually when you don't need them.

It was far too early to be thinking about bivvying, so I tucked my water bottle away, rubbed on some sun cream (in April!) and set out along the track.

I had not seen another human being since the pub on the A road and my isolation only served to intensify the experience of being outdoors in such glorious weather, crossing such fine countryside.

I started uphill again, passing the old boundary stones. The view opened out and the huge sweep of Stanage Edge lay in front of me. The path follows quite near the edge and I took my time walking along it, so that I could savour the view.

I passed strange little bowls, chiselled into the rock by Edwardian gamekeepers to collect rainwater for pheasants to drink, each one carefully marked with its own identifying number carved next to it. I wondered how many were originally carved and how many of them survived today, and if it might be possible to map them so that people might walk them and tick them off if they wanted to, like Munros[2] but without the height gain. So nothing like Munros then, since the uphill and downhill are the essential, defining part of Munro bagging.

Next were some old millstones, quarried from the rock face but never used and abandoned *in situ*. When I got back to work, I was asked about my trip and I showed a picture of the millstones, explaining what they were. One woman commented, "Yes, and look at all those wheels someone's abandoned as well". History according to the Flintstones.

I was getting tired and thirsty. I knew I had enough water for dinner that evening and breakfast tomorrow, provided that I didn't guzzle lots of it here and now. So, with the promise of "jam tomorrow", it was time to start looking for a suitable bivvy site.

A good view was an important criterion, but a good view was pretty much guaranteed wherever I camped up here, in this weather.

I needed a flat piece of ground, at least as big as myself. Most importantly of all I wanted it to be away from other people.

That last stipulation is not due to any misanthropy on my part. Well, not entirely. It's mostly because I am going to lie down and go to sleep up here, and I don't want anyone messing about with me or my kit while I do so.

There is also an element of respect for whoever owns the land. When I camp I leave no trace, and I mean no trace. Not so much as a burnt match. The last

---

[2] Munros: Scottish mountains over 3,000 feet high, originally listed by Sir Hugh Munro in 1891. The practice of climbing them is known as "Munro bagging".

thing I do before I leave any place where I have camped is a "paper chase", a slow walk back and forth across the plot to find and remove anything that I might otherwise inadvertently leave behind. I take pride in the fact that when I've camped somewhere you would be hard pressed to find any evidence of that fact. A dog might notice that someone had been there, but a person wouldn't.

That enthusiasm for being unobtrusive extends not just to the time when I leave, but also to the time when I'm camping. I think it's a fair assumption that when landowners, other walkers, day trippers, or anyone else using the land casts their eye across it, the first thing they want to see is not yours truly cluttering up the view. I guess it's just a basic respect for other people; so we started at misanthropy and ended up at completely the other end of the spectrum.

Some of the better-looking bivvy sites were just a bit too close to the edge for my liking. If the local after-pub crowd didn't roll me and my bivvy bag over the edge in the night for a laugh, I could imagine myself turning over in the night and rolling off.

Unsurprisingly, as I got fussier the number of potential sites got fewer.

I needed to get away from the climbers and boulderers. Is "boulderers" a noun, I mused? It must be if "boulder" is a verb, which it has become in recent years. Anyway, people were climbing and bouldering and I wanted a little more solitude. In particular, I didn't want to have to listen to the chinking of their carabiners and camming devices, getting inexorably louder until one of them popped his head above the cliff edge right next to my bivvy.

So I wandered on a little further and eventually decided to stop wandering and to stake a claim for my bit of Stanage Edge, and wait them out. After all, I was going to be here all night. The boulderers and picnickers would have to give up and go home sooner or later.

I found what looked like an ideal spot: a rock overhang in case of bad weather with a flat, good-sized piece of ground right underneath it.

I sat down and made a cup of tea, looking out across the Derwent Valley towards Offerton Moor.

To my left was a higher outcrop of rock. Two young lads were climbing it in jeans and trainers, apparently to impress a girl who sat at the foot of the rocks and minded their cache of bottles of lager. I was only a matter of metres away, but not one of them seemed to realise I was there.

While his mate slowly clambered higher, one of the boys gave it up and climbed down to re-join the girl. Maybe that was his plan all along: keep his not-too-bright mate occupied while he made his move on the love interest.

The remaining climber had slowed but kept going towards the top. The challenge he'd chosen was not a huge climb, but it was high enough to result in life-changing injury if he fell. It occurred to me that if the silly sod did fall off, I was probably the only person there with enough wit to know what to do next. Selfishly, it also occurred to me that this would spoil my weekend, so I silently wished the climber well.

The land to my right didn't rise as much, and coming from there, I could hear the chink and clink of proper climbers, interspersed by the occasional terse comment.

I sipped my tea and watched the sun drop to the western horizon. I didn't really care what the weather would be like tomorrow. Today had been so glorious that I felt I was happy to pay the price for it by enduring however many rainy days equalled one sunny day. I loosened my boots and wiggled my feet.

There was no need to give away my intention too early, and as I've already described, I like to keep my camping low-profile, so I started to get my dinner. If anyone asked I could always deny an intent to camp here; after all, I hadn't unpacked any sleeping gear. I could quite reasonably argue that I was simply going to have something to eat and then move on. Where's the harm in that?

Of course, if I ever did have that conversation I would probably have to move on after eating, so I was quite keen not to have it in the first place.

To my left, Derbyshire's answer to Edmund Hillary reached the top of his climb (fair play to him) only to find that his friends had walked around and were now sitting at the top waiting for him, and drinking the lager. His mate had made shrewd use of his time alone with the girl and he now sat with his arm around her, nuzzling her neck. Bizarrely the girl seemed to respond better to personal attention than to rock climbing. Women, eh? Will we ever understand them?

The climbing-expert / muppet-at-romance accepted the last bottle of lager and sat at their feet, playing gooseberry.

To my right the climbers had packed up and silence was beginning to fall.

The kids to my left started singing. I thought they would soon run out of songs, or willpower, but not a bit of it. I thought about asking them to pack it in, but what the hell? They weren't hurting anybody and it seemed unlikely that they would be here all night. That thought made me remember an old joke:

"My great-grandfather was killed at the Battle of Little Bighorn. He wasn't involved in the fighting; he

was camping nearby and he'd gone over to complain about the noise."

I smiled and unrolled my sleeping mat. The two lads and the girl gathered up their empties (fair play again) and began slowly wending their way down the hill. I sorted out my sleeping arrangements and watched the sky and the land slowly change colour from the comfort of my bivvy bag.

Bivvy bagging is an attractive alternative to tent camping, but I would argue that it is just that, an alternative. It's not necessarily better or worse, just different.

The main advantage of a tent is that it provides more sheltered space than a bivvy bag. A tent provides more room in which to cook, eat, wash, change clothes and so on. A bivvy bag on the other hand provides a connection with the land like no other. There is often little weight saving, because advances in tent design and fabrics mean that there are many one-person backpacking tents of similar weight to bivvy bags. But a bivvy bag can allow you views of the night sky that have to be seen to be believed and, provided you select an appropriate colour, a bivvy bag is very low profile. While a tent is always a tent, a bivvy bag can easily be positioned so that it is impossible for the casual passer-by to notice.

The knack to using any type of bivvy bag, assuming reasonably sensible campsite selection, is controlling condensation on the inside of the bag. That condensation originates with you, the occupant. Some condensation from bodily moisture is inevitable, but this is usually minimal and should not cause a problem. The most problematic source of moisture inside the bag is condensation from your breath, so it is necessary to stress one simple rule:

Do not exhale into the bivvy bag!

If you do, you will wake up with a surprising amount of water pooled in your bag, even to the extent that you convince yourself the bag must be leaking. But the cause is almost always your breath.

Given, then, that when you breathe out, you must do so out of the bag not into it, the most important skill for successful camping lies in finding a method by which you can exhale out of the bag while still keeping your face warm and dry. The practicality (or impracticality) of this exercise should be one of the principal factors you consider when assessing the suitability of the different types and models of bivvy bag. If you buy a bag that is designed so that in bad weather you must seal it up and breathe into it, you will get wet.

Of the different models available, my favourite is the type that has an opening at the head end controlled by a drawstring. Using this type of bag in bad weather it's possible, with a little practice, to draw in the string and create a very small breathing hole, and then to arrange the material of the bag above the hole to prevent rain coming in. This system has the beauty that you can move about as much as you like in the night and take the breathing hole with you as you do so. Other types of bag, with hoods or zips, don't always let you do this.

The next morning I drifted back into consciousness slowly and gently, gradually becoming aware of the rising sun and the mist on the lower ground. It was a morning of stunning beauty, completely still and yet changing and developing into what would obviously be a splendid day.

I was up and eating my breakfast, watching dawn's metamorphosis into day, while most people were still sunk in slumber.

I broke camp with a spring in my step and I'd made several miles and explored the majestic Iron Age hill fort of Carl Wark before I met another person. Then it was all downhill, across fields, through woods and early spring bulbs, back to my start point.

But it wasn't always to be as good or as straightforward.

----- x -----

Chapter 2
Dartmoor

"An inconvenience is an adventure wrongly considered."

G. K. Chesterton

It was a lovely day as Giles, Neil, Walt and I left the car at the old Okehampton railway station and shouldered our packs. We crossed the A30 dual carriageway by the footbridge, the good weather buoying up our spirits as much as the traffic noise tried to drag them back down.

The noise faded into the background as we made our way up the East Okement River, sunlight filtering through the trees but the new leaves providing just enough shade as we gained height. We soon stepped out into the sunshine and onto the moor, heading south. Just looking across the almost featureless ground ahead reminded me how difficult navigation could be if the weather closed in.

We passed Scarey Tor (it wasn't) and skirted the MoD Danger Area until we reached Oke Tor. If we positioned ourselves well at Oke Tor, the huge piles of fractured granite would protect us from the wind.

Tents up, we set about making hot drinks, and it was at this point that I proudly produced my new lightweight stove.

At that time, I had just started down the road of lightweight backpacking and for me it was a gradual process. At least it was at first. I thought I'd replace older kit as it wore out and my plan was to replace it with lighter kit. So my clunky old gas stove had given way to a sleek little number, weighing in at a mere 77g.

Giles has never grasped the lightweight concept and when I'd met him at his house earlier that day I'd ribbed him mercilessly about the huge size and weight of his rucksack, and I'd continued to stick it to him as he'd struggled and sweated his way across the moor.

The stove had looked a bit flimsy at home and here "on the hill", where I had to rely on it, it looked flimsier still. Several parts of it that I would have expected to be made of metal were, in fact, made of plastic, and I started to wonder whether it would be man enough for the job. It had been reassuringly expensive, but the word "robust" did not spring readily to mind. I reminded myself that lightweight kit was never going to look or feel as if it was built like a tank: that would be a contradiction in terms.

So I proudly showed off my new stove, then screwed it to a gas cylinder and fired it up. It boiled water quickly and efficiently, and I was soon drinking tea and chatting with my mates.

With the tea drunk, the evening drawing in and the temperature dropping, it was time to get dinner. I set up my new stove behind some low rocks, re-positioned the even-more-lightweight windshield around it, and lit it up to heat a main meal. With everything in place, I wandered over for a chat with one of the others and after a few minutes I wandered back, to see how dinner was progressing. I didn't get dinner, but I did get quite a surprise.

The stove was roaring like a jet engine. It didn't look quite like it had when I'd made tea only a short while ago and it took a second or so of staring at it before I realised what I was seeing. The gas burner at the stop of the stove was spouting a huge yellow flame that was enveloping the pot perched on top of it. Underneath the loud roaring of the burner, almost in the background, I could hear a hissing noise and at first I couldn't work out quite where it was coming from. Then I noticed the flames burning aggressively up the sides of the stove unit, just above the point at which it was screwed into the gas canister. The gas was coming out of the join with such force that the flame wasn't visible until a further two inches up the stove stem. More flames were shooting out of what used to be the flame adjustment knob.

What happened next took the merest fraction of a second to act out but takes considerably longer than that to relate.

The whole ensemble looked as if it could explode at any moment. Clearly, my initial priority must be to create as much distance as I could between me and the stove. Ideally between all of us and the stove. I had the surreal thought that the best way to achieve this would be to post the thing to America, but surrealism felt like an indulgence I couldn't afford.

There was no time to shout a warning to the others and then follow up the inevitable demands for explanation. I had nothing I could throw over the stove to smother it. If I couldn't turn the stove off or quickly move my colleagues further away from it, my only option was to move the stove and my mind raced to work out how I might achieve this.

Sling it. But don't spill boiling water over yourself in the process. I grabbed a glove (no time to put it on) and used it to shield my hand from the roaring flame as I removed the pot of boiling water as quickly as I could without spilling it.

With the boiling water rendered safe, I moved on to the stove and the gas canister. Using the glove as a sort of oven mitt, I tried to lift the roaring stove by the canister, near the base, but it didn't work. Something was making the canister slippery and it kept jumping out of my grip like a bar of soap in the bath.

I'd got rid of the pan of boiling water and there was only the crippled stove and the gas reservoir left to deal with. My subconscious had ditched surrealism but had gone too far the other way towards realism: "Out of the frying pan into the fire", my mind kept telling me. I forced myself to focus on the fire in front of me. The glove started smouldering and I threw it to one side. I grabbed the gas canister with my right hand and lifted it off the ground, with the roaring stove still attached, just above my hand.

The instant I touched the canister with my bare hand I realised why it was slippery: it was covered in a film of ice. As I lifted it, my hand also became covered in ice and I realised that the gas shooting out of the cylinder and the stove assembly was freezing onto my hand. A strange phenomenon and one that would have been interesting to consider more fully had the circumstances been less pressing. However, it struck me that whatever was frozen onto my hand might still ignite, so I quickly cocked my arm and hurled the fireball as far away as I could.

Walt, busy cooking his own dinner nearby, had witnessed the whole thing. Sometime afterwards, in the pub, he described it thus, "You know how the space shuttle looks when it re-enters the Earth's atmosphere? Well, it was like that but with more swearing."

I took stock of what I had left. A pot, a windshield and a lingering sense of injustice about summed it up. It looked like I'd be eating my food cold for the next few days. Either that or go home early.

Luckily for me, Neil offered me the use of his stove, an act far more generous than it sounds because he didn't know if he would have enough gas for both of us. It's in times of adversity that you find out who your friends are and I'm still grateful.

Then Giles revealed to us why his rucksack was so big and so heavy: it was his birthday a few days before this trip and he had filled his rucksack with cans of beer for us to drink in celebration while we were camping. I have never made a dig about heavy gear since then.

After I got home, I took the burnt-out stove back to the shop I'd bought it from and asked for a refund. My mood was not improved by the response I got: "No-one else has had that problem".

"No-one else has complained". The motto of poor customer service the world over. If you work in any service industry, consider this: how the hell does the fact that no one else has complained have anything to do with the complaint in front of you? Why not just call me names and be done with it? Or is there just the faintest glimmer of a possibility that we could banish this phrase once and for all? Customer service at any level would be better for its total absence.

Next, the assistant suggested operator error. I countered with the fact that the same set up which got so out of hand had neatly and efficiently boiled water for tea just a few minutes earlier. I had kept it assembled and the only things I'd done were to turn it back on and light it again.

Operator error! I couldn't resist adding that I've been backpacking for 30 years and during that time I've used almost every type of stove imaginable. Never once have I needed the help of Red Adair to get my dinner.

After a bit more verbal to-ing and fro-ing they grudgingly offered to send it back to the makers and see what they said. I had to return in ten weeks for a decision.

I left the shop feeling as if I had been released from a police station on bail, and made my way to another shop to buy a new stove. Ten weeks later they gave me my money back.

Putting self-immolation to one side, what other cooking options are available?

There are probably more types and sizes of stove available today than there ever have been. And just about all of them are good in their own way. Like so many things, it's just a question of working out what is best for you.

Firstly, give some thought to what you want your stove to do. That sounds like a no-brainer, but most people's needs do vary.

If you make up dehydrated meals then all you will need to do is boil water.

If you heat "boil in foil" meals then you need a stove that will boil water quickly and that has sufficient control flexibility to simmer for a while.

And if you like to cook meals from ingredients you'll need a stove that gives you even more control over temperature.

Next up, how many people's food will be prepared on your stove? If you are going to share, make sure your stove is big enough for the job.

So, having thought about the types of food and drink you'll be preparing, and the number of people involved, you're in a position to consider the main types of stove: gas, meths, biomass, solid fuel or multi-fuel.

Gas canister stoves are convenient and reliable. They can also be very light. Canister types can vary from country to country so check before you travel. It is possible to find adaptors, with a little searching on the Internet, so you can give yourself some flexibility and be able to adapt your stove for other canister types. Just don't try to take gas canisters onto aeroplanes; this is one battle the terrorists have already won.

Gas stoves can be sluggish in cold weather – if necessary warm the canister by placing it in your clothes or sleeping bag.

Methylated spirit stoves tend to be even lighter than gas canister stoves, although some older models are still quite hefty. Meths is widely available. Again, it's not allowed on planes. Don't ask me why not, it's no more flammable than your duty free bottle of brandy.

However, meths stoves take much longer to boil water than gas stoves and if you need simmer control, you'll have to find it through trial and error.

"Biomass" is the trendy name for wood and there are some really innovative wood stove designs that have become available, some of them very lightweight. The best ones work on a handful of twigs and can generate a surprising amount of heat. Fuel for biomass stoves is readily available and free, and they circumvent the air travel dilemma: just arrive at your destination and pick up some fuel while you're walking. The key here is to select "air-dried" twigs, i.e. those that have become detached from their host tree, but which have become lodged on another branch or twig and so have dried somewhat as a result. Twigs on the ground will very often be damp.

The drawback of wood-burning stoves is the residue, a sort of black, sooty, tarry deposit. Your pot gets black and your stove gets black. Surprisingly quickly, your hands get black too. And this stuff is the devil to wash off, in fact it's just about impossible to remove it completely from your hands in the field: some of it always seems to remain between the whorls on your fingertips or round your fingernails. And you'll smell like a tramp.

There is, however, something very primal and instinctively satisfying about using a fire.

Solid fuel hexamine tablets are available in most camping shops. They cook much like meths does: once lit you can't adjust the flame and they are not easy to extinguish and re-use, so you don't get the on/off flexibility you have with gas and simmer control is not easily achieved. But they are light, and some of the smaller solid fuel stoves weigh literally just a few grams. Add in a small foil windshield and you have a very lightweight set up.

Be wary of the traditional armed forces hexy stoves: while they are widely available, they are heavy and they don't come with the much-needed windshield.

Multi-fuel stoves are useful for extended trips across long distances because they give you a choice of fuel sources (e.g. diesel, paraffin, petrol or gas). They tend to weigh more than some other options and can need servicing, albeit self-servicing.

----- x -----

Chapter 3
Cherill Down, Wiltshire

"If I could not walk far and fast, I think I should just explode and perish."
                                                    Charles Dickens

Sometimes it's difficult to get away.

Sometimes it's hard to free up the time to get outdoors, particularly if your time off has to coincide with your mates' time off. Before you know it, you find yourself walking to the station each morning, wondering what it would be like if you were walking in the hills instead. You realise that it has been *ages* since you last got out and about. Slowly but surely the itch starts to build up.

The Cherill Down trip was a one-nighter, specifically organised to scratch that itch. We set out across the Wiltshire downs, off into the murk of an autumn day. The weather was nothing special and, as a consequence, neither were the views. But who cared? We were outside and we were walking.

The going got sticky at one point as we slopped and slurped down a farm track whipped into watery mud by recreational 4x4s. What is the matter with these people? What pleasure do they get tanking along converting the paths and bridleways to liquid slop, making them impassable to their intended users? These nuisances really need to be put in their place, so when I hear them coming up behind me, I get into the middle of the track and stay there as long as I can. Slows them right down. It's not much, but if we all did it, they might get the message. A single act of defiance is worth a thousand angry words and all that.

Anyway, after a good day's walk we crossed a main road, and gained some height up a chalk farm track. When the track had taken us a fair way from the road, we turned off it and walked a reasonable distance away. We are almost obsessive about leaving no trace when we camp, but landowners who might see us don't know that. Better for everyone to be unobtrusive and avoid confrontation in the first place.

So, finally satisfied that we were in the middle of nowhere, we found a clearing and pitched camp. As I put my tent up, I considered the Law of Tents, developed by my friend John Walters to explain the relationship between a man and his tents. The Law of Tents is expressed by the formula:

$$t = n + 1$$

where t = the ideal number of tents for any given man and n = the number of tents he currently owns. A female friend tells me that a similar formula operates to explain the relationship between women and shoes, but the least said on that subject the better.

After dinner, we spent a sociable evening around a roaring fire and then turned in.

I was woken up prematurely at about 1am by what sounded like all hell breaking loose. There were loud, sporadic crashes and bangs, and multi-coloured lights flashing all around us. Half-dazed and half-asleep, I blundered out of my sleeping bag and stumbled out of my tent, boots undone and clutching my pocket-knife (which I'd forgotten to open), ready to repel the attackers who, I was convinced, must be among us.

There was no one around our tents. My next thought was that we must have blundered into some sort of Army battle training exercise, but the lights and the noise looked more like huge industrial fireworks.

I did a quick mental calculation to work out which of my companions would be most likely to hide large fireworks in his rucksack, carry them all day and then sneak out in the dead of night to let them off and scare the hell out of the rest of us. Any of them, quite frankly. So that didn't take me much further forward.

The other tents were firmly closed while bangs and flashes erupted from the trees around us, and crescendoed overhead.

I didn't think the culprit would have been able to light them all and get back inside his tent before I came out of mine, so I did a check on the other tents. Everyone was where they should have been and one or two voices quavered a little. Unless they had developed good acting skills overnight, they were as surprised as I was.

I considered the idea that they were all responsible, but I doubted that they could coordinate themselves sufficiently to carry it off.

As suddenly as they had started, the fireworks stopped. The woods reverted to their original pitch-blackness, still and silent, made ominous now by what had just happened. There was thick undergrowth around us with barbed wire fences in it at some points. It would have been very difficult to move through that without either using a light or making noise. But the night was as still as if the fireworks had never happened.

I concluded that whoever had set them off had made his getaway immediately after lighting them, or I would have seen or heard him. I didn't think he'd still be in situ: he'd know we'd be ready if he kicked off Round 2.

At dawn, we crawled out of our tents, stretched and began the process of getting breakfast and discussing the night's events. We found the carcasses of last night's fireworks and I quickly realised that none of my friends could have smuggled them in their rucksacks the previous day and remained undetected: each one was about the size of a case of wine and there were lots of them. But as we packed up it quickly became apparent that one person, while not directly responsible, knew more than he should.

James had arranged for a friend to meet us mid-morning at the end of our walk and drive us back to our start point. They'd had a conversation by text late the previous evening and James had disclosed our location in the form of a six-figure grid reference. Michael, his friend, had happily gone to bed that night, but had set his alarm clock to wake him many hours earlier than he normally would. He'd got up in the wee hours, loaded his Land Rover with big commercial fireworks and navigated his way out to us. Then he'd toted the fireworks through the woods, set them up and lit the fuses, and made good his escape using the mayhem he had just created as cover.

We met Michael just a short while later when he came back to collect us in his 4x4. I'll admit to a grudging respect for a man who will go to so much trouble just to scare the living crap out of his mates and a few people he's never met. And it was good of him to act as a taxi service for us, although we could have made much better speed back to the main road if we hadn't encountered walkers loitering in the middle of the track at every turn. I suppose more are likely to turn out at weekends, but most of them looked half-asleep and didn't seem to realise we were coming until we were right on their heels. It's not as if they need the whole width of the track either, but so many of them don't even have the wit to walk along the side. There is almost a dumb insolence to some of them and I have to say that Michael was far more tolerant of them than I would have been if I were driving.

----- x -----

Chapter 4
The West Highland Way

"I have two doctors, my left leg and my right."
George Macauley Trevelyan

The alarm goes at 0315. The world is still in darkness but I'm out of bed in a second. I check the news on television, have a quick wash and a quicker breakfast, and I'm ready to go. There is good reason for my enthusiasm.

My minicab to the bus station is booked for 0415. At 0410 I am outside my house with my rucksack on the road beside me, but 0415 comes and goes with no sign of a taxi.

I hate lateness, but minicabs don't, in my limited experience of them, usually operate to the same level of punctuality that I do.

I hate lateness and I will not be late, especially today. The Close is quiet and in darkness, including my house.

I hate lateness. At 0425 I snap, unlock the front door, go back in, turn the lights back on and telephone the minicab firm.

"It's on the way."

Sure it is. I imagine the next conversation in the minicab office went something along the lines of, "Put that tea down, you're supposed to be picking up that bloke in Langdon Hills."

At 0428 the cab arrives and I get to the bus station at 0435, in plenty of time for my 0450 bus to Stansted Airport.

The bus station is in the centre of town, which is completely deserted. It's a good feeling to do the occasional early start, for my own purposes, not for work of course. No one is up but me and I am up for a good reason. I'm off to walk the West Highland Way with some friends.

This trip has been months in the planning and even longer in the anticipation. And now it has started.

But the problem with Scotland, if you live in the south-east of England, is getting there. We had booked cheap flights and flying is quick, but not so much so when you add in the mandatory two hour early arrival so that you can check in, and the fact that you've still got to get from the airport to your destination. And you can't carry the gas canisters you need to fuel your camping stove, oh no, that would allow the terrorists to win. So you also have to allow enough time to scour Scotland for gas.

The first problem was getting to the airport.

I could have driven there, but then I would have had to fork out for parking fees. A few days ago, a leaflet had appeared through my letter box telling me how a bus company would take me to the airport from the centre of my town for a mere £16 return. I'd booked my ticket and got myself to the bus station in plenty of time. I felt that I'd done my part of the deal, now over to the bus company. But where was the bus?

The bus arrived 10 minutes late, at 0500, the driver eager to explain the difficulties of negotiating roadworks, and the shortcomings of his company in failing to adapt the timetables to reflect this. He hadn't yet completed his outbound journey but he was going to turn back from this point and take me to Stansted. He was an amiable man, Scottish, and when I mentioned the purpose of my journey, keen to chat.

As I arrived at the airport, I received a good luck text from my son. The lump in my throat caused by this delayed the phone call to my mum to wish her a happy birthday, but only by a few minutes.

And in just a few hours, obviously via a number of outdoor shops in Glasgow to find gas, I found myself at Milngavie, the start of the West Highland Way, along with Giles, Walt and Nick. It was a beautiful, dry, sunny day, with just a few white clouds scudding across a bright blue sky as we gathered at the starting point in the main shopping street.

The West Highland Way was formally opened in 1980 and it was Scotland's first official long-distance footpath. It's 155km long, or 96 miles in old money. Depending on whom you consult, between 30,000 and 70,000 people complete the Way each year.

For us it was time to kit up. This happens at the start of every trip but I never quite get used to it. Adjusting my clothes and changing my walking kit from travel mode to "on-the-hill" mode takes just a few minutes, but every time I do it, it seems to emphasise the frailty of individual human beings and the enormity of the outdoors. Am I really going to live comfortably and thrive with so few, flimsy items?

For better or worse, I know that I am. So I slipped the caps off my walking poles and off we went.

For me a long-distance walk only really starts when I take the rubber caps off the ends of my trekking poles. I usually keep them on through the town, because the "click-click" of metal pole tips on tarmac or concrete creates a disturbance that seems to me to be unnecessary. The obvious flip side is, of course, that when I put them back on again as I meet tarmac at journey's end, the walk is emphatically over.

----- x -----

We stopped for a beer at The Beech Tree Inn at Dumgoyne and it was there that we first met The Most Boring Man in the World.

His real name was Reg. We'd spotted Reg some miles back, labouring along underneath an Army style 100 litre rucksack (full), wearing Army trousers (similarly full). Close up we could see that he liked his Army kit: he was even wearing an Army watch. I have nothing against Army kit, but I tend not to use it because they make it to be more robust than I need it to be and robust equals heavy. My kit is not going to be dumped out of a helicopter or rattled around inside a tank, so I can get away with much lighter stuff. And not everyone wants to look as if they're Army-barmy.

Reg started by asking us how far we'd walked. At that point, we had no idea of the trap yawning open before us and we stepped right into it. We quickly discovered that conversation, to Reg, meant other people listening while he talked. About himself. So the opener, "How far have you walked today?" quickly became a monologue about how far Reg had walked. Over 20 miles, in case you're interested. Next, "What make of rucksack have you got there?" immediately became a long recommendation for his own rucksack.

Mistaking the fact that we hadn't beaten him with sticks as evidence of our enthusiasm for more, Reg careered merrily into his life history, extolling the virtues of early retirement, "You've got to get out before the stress hits". I tried not to visualise his old workmates reminiscing about how much more pleasurable work had become since their stress had taken early retirement.

There was only so much of this nonsense we could take, so when Reg took a rare pause for breath, we quickly made our excuses and legged it.

----- x -----

That evening we stopped to camp at a pleasant little campsite at Gartness, next to an old railway line, behind what looked like a village hall.

The "village hall" turned out to be some sort of function room with pretty Scotch waitresses who sold us cider on the condition that we also bought cake, to comply with the terms of their liquor licence. I hadn't seen most of the lads since my birthday a month or so ago, so I bought the cake as my birthday cake with the cider on the side.

It was a glorious early evening with the clear blue sky portending a crisp night to come. Mellowed by the cider, the cake, a shower and toilet facilities, we contemplated a leisurely dinner while watching the sun set.

And at that precise moment, an Army 100 litre rucksack powered onto the site. Closer inspection revealed The Most Boring Man in the World underneath it.

Walt muttered, "It's early yet, he'll keep on going", but he didn't. He came straight for us like some sort of guided missile and greeted us like long-lost friends.

He asked us how we'd found the last few miles of walking, but before we could answer he was telling us at length how marvellous his trekking poles were.

I try to be moderate in my attitude towards other people. After all, the world would be a pretty boring place if we were all alike, and I'm mature enough (I think) to recognise that it would be completely uninhabitable if everyone was like me. But this was dragging down the trip right from the beginning. It led to some, for me, unusually intemperate language in my diary that evening.

I put Reg out of my mind and snuggled into my down sleeping bag, drifting off to sleep with the tent flap open so I could enjoy the sunset, and thinking about my children.

As predicted, the price for that sunny day and clear sky was a cold night. I didn't feel it, tucked away in my cosy sleeping bag, but the temperature dropped well below freezing and my tent was stiff with ice as I made breakfast.

More importantly, we managed to leave Reg behind as we set off for Drymen.

We stopped for coffee, Nick and I, at a campsite a few miles through the forest. It was bland and inoffensive enough (the coffee, not the campsite) and served over the counter in bendy plastic cups, like the ones excreted by vending machines. It didn't feel quite right to me. We'd only been on the trail for a short while but we were already men set apart from civilisation, particularly civilisation in the form of crappy plastic cups.

We were out of sight of Giles and Walt as we got to Drymen, so we stopped for a cup of tea and a sticky while they caught us up. But then they wanted tea and cake, so there was still a gap between us as Nick and I finished our elevenses and set off again.

Passing through Garadhban Forest as the day went on, enjoying the sunshine, I started wondering just how hot it would get in early May. I've since realised that, contrary to the accepted wisdom, Scotland has a Mediterranean climate. On the few occasions I've been there, it has been resolutely warm and sunny. I've come to the conclusion that it's always like that and the Scots actively promote the idea that they have bad weather purely to keep the place for themselves. Obviously they don't want the beaches getting too crowded.

Nick and I got wise to this after a couple of trips. Now when we pass the time of day with a local in Scotland and he sounds off about how harsh the winter was, we nod conspiratorially and go along with the deception. When the pub barmaid expresses surprise at the unseasonal sunshine, we smile and remark that it must be a nice change. But we know.

On the far edge of the forest, we crossed some moorland on the approach to Conic Hill, where we paused. I glanced at my phone and saw that I had a signal, so I thought I'd check on progress with Walt and Giles.

Walt's assertions that they were just coming through the forest seemed to indicate that they weren't far behind. Nick suggested lunch while we waited for them to catch us up, so we sprawled in the sunshine, packs off, lightening our loads by eating part of them.

After half an hour of this, I tried Walt again. Still coming through the forest, apparently. There was a note in his voice that didn't sound quite right, but I couldn't put my finger on it and I thought no more about it.

Several people had already passed us by this stage and as each appeared at the forest edge in the distance and began walking towards us, Nick and I strained our eyes to see if our brains could transform the distant shapes into Giles and Walt. But none of them were.

After an hour, so many people had passed us that I was starting to feel less like a walker and more like some sort of long-distance picnicker. Nick and I decided that the other two couldn't miss the correct route, so we swung our packs on with (by now) practised ease and set off once more, up the steep climb that is the east side of Conic Hill.

I got to the top first and sat there with the day-trippers, drinking in the view of Loch Lomond on the other side, waiting for Nick to join me.

The top of Conic Hill gave a good view back over our route and it was now obvious that, whatever Giles and Walt were doing, they weren't climbing Conic Hill.

After a brief discussion, we concluded that they'd probably taken the B road around the base of the hill, a sensible route if they were struggling, but obviously as Nick and I were now seasoned hill climbers, we looked forward to taking the Mickey at the first opportunity.

Pictures taken, sated with the view, Nick and I made our way down the steep slope towards the visitor centre, the prospect of unlimited ice cream and water giving a spring to our stride.

In the car park was a toilet, an ice cream van and all the water we could drink. And Giles and Walt.

After checking that everyone was all right, the inevitable question, "Did you take the B road?"

"The B road? Yeah, that's right." That note in Walt's voice again. Hmm.

But we had more immediate concerns to attend to. One ice cream later and it was on to The Oak Tree

Inn in Balmaha. The pub was packed with trippers but it was too enticing a prospect to pass up, so it was inside for a few pints and a large dinner. Quite a smart restaurant for us scruffy hikers, but they managed to fit us in and they did us proud with food and drink.

After a few more beers, I raised the route issue again.

"You must have done a similar distance to us along the B road, just without the up and down."

"Well", a pause, "We did go along the B road." Walt looked sheepish. "But we got the bus."

Brilliant! Nick and I had been looking for the right moment to rub in the fact that Walt and Giles had wimped out of the hilly bit, but finding out they'd wimped out of walking altogether was manna from heaven. We exploited this moral advantage to the maximum, had another drink and then pushed it home some more.

Only when Nick and I were satisfied that we had extracted every possible ounce of humour and degradation from the situation did we put our glasses down, shoulder our packs and get back on the West Highland Way.

----- x -----

The section of the Way that runs alongside the shore of Loch Lomond almost put me off the entire experience. Wherever we looked, there were empty beer cans and barbecue trash. In places the drinkers and eaters had even bagged up their rubbish and then left it in huge heaps for someone else (God knows who) to remove. I had left the guidebook at home to save weight, but I recalled that the author described this part of the trail as, "Scotland's national disgrace". I was glad someone shared my annoyance.

But what annoyed me even more was the response of the authorities. The response of The Loch Lomond and The Trossachs National Park Authority to the extensive littering along the eastern shore of Loch Lomond has been to ban camping.

Yes, you read that correctly: they have banned camping. This struck me as utterly bizarre. Surely, I reasoned as I trudged through the bin liners and scorched disposable barbecues, it would have made more sense to ban littering? After all, not all campers litter, but every litterer does, by definition.

I stepped around a pile of used lager cans and considered that littering *has* been illegal for years. So why not simply enforce the law? Why penalise "leave no trace" campers like me, Giles, Walt and Nick? Why tar us with the same brush?

The more I thought about it the angrier I got, my rising ire fuelled by the open landfill site I was walking through. Who suffers most from the actions of the litter louts of west Scotland? The likes of me, come here for the scenery, that's who. And now I'm criminalised too, by the taxpayer-funded buffoons who should be resolving this problem.

Mind you, if the national park authorities enforce their no camping ban with the same alacrity with which they enforce the litter laws, we won't have much to worry about.

----- x -----

Eventually sheer, dogged persistence saw us out of the Trash Belt and into happier climes.

I was keen to wild camp but I had to agree with the others: Milarrochy Campsite looked a nice place to stop. Spacious pitches, clean toilets, pleasant views of the loch and, perhaps best of all, no Reg. What's not to like? So I shut up. We paid our fees, found our pitches and got the tents up.

I'd put my tent up, sorted my kit out to my satisfaction, and was just straightening up, anticipating another stare at the view and thinking good thoughts, when an all too familiar voice chimed, "Hello lads!" and Reg sauntered in amongst us. I don't know whether he'd arrived before us or as we were pitching our tents, but at least he'd put his up some distance away. I just had time to mumble something about going for water and made off towards the tap, leaving Reg regaling the others with stories about himself and his kit.

As I rounded the corner of the toilet block heading for the kitchen area, I saw four men who stood out from the usual run of campers and caravanners. My first impression was that there must be a Motorhead concert nearby. Then I saw the knives. The men all looked to be in their 40s, with long, lank hair, smoking thin roll-ups and showing a slightly worn appearance. When I was a kid, we would have called them grebos: four low-budget Lemmys, but I noticed that each of them carried a knife in a sheath fixed to his belt.

I can be specific about the knives because I had considered buying the same make of knife before this trip. Because of the ban on carrying gas cartridges on aeroplanes, I'd bought a wood burning camping stove, and a decent knife to prepare the wood had seemed a good idea. Most bushcraft sites recommend this type of knife: high quality and affordable, but the problem for me was that it has a fixed blade four inches long. Section 139 of the Criminal Justice Act 1988 makes it a criminal offence to possess such a knife in a public place without lawful authority or reasonable excuse.

Of course, the Criminal Justice Act applies only to England and Wales, not to Scotland, but I had to cross England to get here. Using the knife to prepare kindling and firewood would probably qualify as "reasonable excuse" but I didn't fancy explaining that to the magistrates. Oh no, the best way to avoid being convicted is to make sure you don't go to court in the first place.

And they could have carried their knives in their rucksacks. I mean, when you decide to do a bit of bushcraft, it's not as if your life depends on getting to your knife quickly.

So the four men were either more convinced of their powers of advocacy than I was or they didn't care. Or they needed their knives readily available.

We exchanged pleasantries as I got my water, and as is so often the case, I found that these people were less threatening than they first appeared. On the other hand, maybe they didn't see me as a threat.

As the evening went on loud music started coming from a caravan-and-awning combination near the top of the site. From where Nick, Giles, Walt and I were camped, with a toilet block and trees between us and the source, it was no more than a mild annoyance, but it must have been a lot louder where the four men were camped.

There were a few raised voices and a few comments shouted across by other caravanners, but the faceless occupants of the caravan and awning just turned up the music and partied on.

There was now what nice people call "an atmosphere" across the campsite and it seemed only a matter of time before some sort of trouble started.

But revenge is a dish best served cold, as we shall see.

----- x -----

Six o'clock the next morning found me awake in my sleeping bag with a rumbling noise coming from the far end of the bag. It was the age-old dilemma of the camper: shall I get out into the cold and head for the toilet or can I last another hour or so? A nice clean toilet block meant that for once there would be no need to find a bush and dig a hole, so I unzipped my sleeping bag.

Morning was breaking as I stepped out of my tent. Everything was fresh with dew and silence reigned. The campsite was still and it felt as if I had the whole world to myself.

I stuffed my wallet and keys into my pocket (never leave your valuables unattended, no matter where), picked up my toilet roll (just in case there wasn't any in the toilet block) and headed for the heads.

I swung open the door to the toilet block, a tune playing in my head, not a care in the world, and got the shock of my life.

There, standing four-square in the middle of the toilet block, was Reg. Not washing. Not coming out of a cubicle. Just standing there. I couldn't escape the impression that he'd stood there all night waiting for me.

"Morning", he commented, as if hanging about in the bogs at 6am was normal behaviour.

If I'd had my wits about me I would have replied, "Doctor Livingstone, I presume?" or something similar. But I didn't, so I just managed a grunt and darted into

Trap 1, slamming the door shut and bolting it a trifle quicker than was strictly necessary.

I briefly debated the probability of Reg coming to join me and decided it was unlikely. Indeed, once I had dropped my trollies and started conducting the South Ockendon Philharmonic, he would have to clear the building, I was in no doubt of that. In the event we never got to test that theory because I'd only got as far as striking up the first few notes when I heard the outer door go and I was alone again.

It would be at least an hour before the others woke up so, refreshed by my trip and vaguely wondering if I'd dreamt Reg in the khazi, I went back to bed.

By about 8 o'clock we were tidying up and getting ready to move off when one of the four men with knives darted from his tent to the caravan that had been the source of last night's noise.

They might have been knocking out a racket last night, but this morning the tired revellers were sunk in slumber. Not a sound came from the caravan, until our hero ran around it, thumping on the walls and windows, shouting, "Come on! Wakey, wakey! Do you like it?!"

Even the most partied-out caravanner would have been woken by this and a slight swaying of the caravan betrayed the hurried movement going on inside. But no response came, absolutely none.

I noticed that the caravan banger did not swear or threaten, and if anyone had called the police, it would have been very difficult to argue that what he was doing constituted an offence. In any case, all the witnesses had been kept awake by the people in the caravan and they were metaphorically right behind him.

He did a second lap of the caravan for luck and wandered back to his mates with a big grin, as peace and a general feeling that justice had been done settled across the campsite.

----- x -----

Arriving at the Rowardennan Hotel at lunchtime was more luck than judgement. Good luck in the case of Giles and Walt, who are both unable to pass a pub without checking it over. Not for their benefit, you understand, purely as a public service.

They were right - it did make sense to stop for a cooked lunch. When you are backpacking, a credit card is always the lightest food to carry, and when we'd originally calculated how much food to bring, we had factored in eating in pubs occasionally.

And here was such a pub, serving food and it was lunchtime. Giles decided the fates must be smiling on him and headed straight through the front door, like a Labrador after a shot pheasant.

The sun came out and we took a table on the patio, drinks in hand, perusing the menu and placing our orders. It was a pleasant spot and it was very easy to have a couple more while the food was being cooked and then, when it arrived, a drop more just to help it down.

When we had finished everything, I got up to go to the Gents. To my surprise, I found I was walking less steadily than I did when we arrived at the pub. The result of walking a long way and then sitting down for too long, I suppose. Funny how even the fittest of people can get taken that way.

As I negotiated the door back into the pub, Giles passed me going the other way with a tray of whiskies. I looked at him, puzzled.

"I thought we were moving on?"

He smiled. "We are. But we need to slow your mate down a bit."

Nick is not the fittest chap around, but he is determined and he will resolutely keep on walking until he gets where he wants to be. Without motor transport, the Bus Boys were having trouble keeping up with him and they'd hatched a plan.

So, as we finished the whiskies, I wasn't entirely surprised to see Walt bringing out a second tray.

I thought they'd let it go at that, but Walt and Giles can also be tenacious when they want to be. I had no sooner stood to pick up my rucksack when Giles emerged from the pub again, this time carrying a tray that held a bottle of red wine and four glasses. The price for slowing down Nick was having to get blotto themselves, but it was a price they were willing to pay.

We drank the wine and chatted. As we finished it, Giles gave me a nudge and indicated Nick.

"There we go."

Nick was lying along a bench seat on his back, with his head hanging off the end and his mouth open.

We each managed to find our own rucksack and put it on, and we made our way back onto the West Highland Way. It was at this point, completely by accident, that I discovered the secret of successful long-distance walking: walk all morning, drink until you can't feel your feet and then walk all afternoon. Sometimes the secrets of inner peace do come to those who meditate long enough.

But the plan had not worked quite as it should have. Nick wasn't much slower and towards teatime, Walt was forced to play his trump card: he showed us his blisters. Now I realise that this sounds a bit feeble, but I couldn't criticise him: they did look decidedly unpleasant. Both heels had large, raw, swollen blisters, punctured and suppurating into his socks. It turned out that Walt had developed these while at work the week before, but he'd still wanted to come walking. His walking boots had made a bad situation much worse and he was now in some pain.

Not to be outdone Giles showed us a blister too, almost big enough to be seen without a magnifying glass.

We sorted out some gel plasters for Walt's blisters and Giles put a supermarket value plaster on his.

Every time we go backpacking, I use a list to help me gather up my kit from its various locations around my home. That way, I always know that I've got everything I need. In case it might save time for others, I usually circulate my list well before the trip. I don't mind whether they use it or not, but at least I don't have to put up with a lot of moaning if they forget anything; I can just retort that, "It was on the list."

Gel plasters are always on my list. I try hard to keep the weight of my kit to a minimum but gel plasters are very light and can make the difference between an enjoyable trip and a Burma Railway experience.

Every time, Giles takes great delight in ignoring the list and in telling me so, so I watched as he stuck what looked like a small cellophane postage stamp over his blister. Predictably, within five paces it had come unstuck and wormed its way around the other side of his sock. Next time I might write "elephant" on the list just to see if he brings a giraffe.

There can be many causes of blisters, and it is especially galling when boots and socks that have hitherto been trustworthy suddenly cause problems. That said, the three main causes of blisters are:

1. Friction;
2. Moisture; and/or,

3. Heat.

Any one of them can cause problems, so control all three of these variables and you have at least a fighting chance of remaining blister-free.

Friction can be the result of too-tight footwear, or because trail debris (grit, bits of twig, etc.) has entered the shoe. Moisture causes the skin to pucker (think of your fingertips after a long bath) and makes it prone to blistering. Heat can cause feet to swell and rub.

Even with his colloidal plasters, Walt wasn't faring much better and it was obvious that we would have to find a campsite soon.

We walked on a little further and found a small beach on Loch Lomond with a rocky promontory, just to the side of the trail. Ideal for a wild camp. The tents went up before we lost the light and we made tea, sitting around a small fire to drink it.

I'd set my tent a little way from the others, just to enjoy a night's sleep free from the sounds of snoring and trumping, and I drifted off to sleep with the tent flap open, watching the moonlight on the loch.

My tactic worked: Nick's tent must have been 50m from me and early the next morning his snoring sounded no louder than a small sawmill.

----- x -----

By about 8 o'clock the next morning Nick and I were fed, washed, packed up and ready to rock. Giles and Walt were still stirring themselves from a chaos of casually strewn pieces of kit. To an uninformed observer they might appear to have slept on a rubbish tip. Or, as Nick describes it, "Their tent looked like a teenager's bedroom".

There was lots of:

"Have you seen my boot?"

"You're holding it."

"Not that one, the other one. I usually wear two."

"How am I supposed to know where your boots are?"

And,

"That sleeping bag was rubbish. I was cold all night."

"You didn't have to keep waking me up to tell me. I got it the first time."

This morning pantomime was hugely entertaining, but we had distance to cover. Nick and I looked at each other. Nick hadn't long met Walt and Giles so it fell to me to put our thoughts into words.

"We're going to crack on. You get yourselves sorted and catch us up. We'll go slowly and stop for coffee."

With that Nick and I slunk off, an animated discussion about which sock belonged to who fading away behind us like mist disappearing in the morning sunshine.

----- x -----

We slogged on along the narrow, stony, rooty path, passing Rob Roy's cave as we did so. It would be difficult to miss the cave, because someone with more enthusiasm than skill has painted the legend "ROB ROYS CAVE" in huge white letters on the rocks.

A triumph of armchair tourism: cruise past on the loch below, fat arse spreading in your hard plastic chair, double-price soft drink at your elbow, and you can tell your children you've seen Rob Roy's Cave. Without even having to reach for the remote.

Below us on the loch, we watched the tourist boat turn and head back, job done, with everyone who wanted to having seen "ROB ROYS CAVE". We turned without a word and walked on. We didn't have to discuss it. Walking was what we were there for.

Inversnaid was a welcome respite. Keen to get properly into the spirit of this lightweight backpacking lark, we got some money out and made straight for the hotel (which was much smarter than we were but they needed our business), and we ordered some lunch.

Walt's fond of saying that, "Hunger is the poor man's sauce", and there is a lot in that simple statement. It's also true, although maybe less compact and less pithy, that day trippers are the trekker's relish; and the addition of a coachload of trippers made our lunch even more enjoyable as we larged it up in front of them while we ate at our table in the mild sunshine.

But movement is the essential element of travel and even backwoodsmen as grizzled as Nick and I could only pose around for so long before it was time to walk again.

----- x -----

All too soon, we found ourselves at the lochside near Ardleish, with Ardlui on the opposite bank. We hadn't made the progress we'd hoped on this trip and our time was up. Giles and Walt had gone to fetch the hire car and the arrangement was that they would meet us in Ardlui, outside the hotel.

Every Day above a New Horizon

I hoisted the orange buoy up the pole to summon the ferry, thinking as I did so that unless the ferryman was sitting on the other side glued to his window we were in for a long wait.

But almost immediately we could make out a small boat setting course towards us from the marina opposite. It was a sad moment because our trip was over, but it was an unusual way to end it.

The ferry tied up at Ardlui and Nick and I stepped off onto the pontoon. We swung our rucksacks on and made our way up to the hotel.

It was tempting to slip inside for a drink but there would be plenty of time for that later. And we had agreed to rendezvous outside the front of the hotel.

Nick and I set down our packs. Nick found a seat and fished out a newspaper; I strolled up and down in front of the hotel building, relishing the feeling of walking without the weight of a rucksack.

After a few minutes the hire car appeared, with Walt and Giles in the front seats. I had anticipated a longer wait so I was impressed with their timing.

I waved both arms, thinking as I did so that the gesture was superfluous: we had agreed to meet outside the front of the Ardlui Hotel and I was the only person standing directly in front of the only building on this stretch of road. A building, moreover, which bore the legend "Ardlui Hotel" in large letters, as if to dispel any doubt.

Walt and Giles sailed past.

They couldn't have missed me; they must have left it too late to pull over.

I waited for the car to turn round and come back. Then I waited some more.

It couldn't take this long.

Eventually the car came back, travelling in the other direction.

Just in case they hadn't seen me on the first pass, I waved both arms over my head again but this time I also jumped up and down to add emphasis. Under the hotel sign.

The car cruised serenely past.

I swore.

Stuff this, I decided. I had been prepared for a long wait for the other two, but once they'd arrived I expected to get on with things. We still had to pitch camp and get cleaned up; there was perfectly good beer in this hotel and it wasn't going to drink itself. I gave up on the idea of signalling to the dynamic duo in the hire car and made my way back to Nick and my rucksack.

Nick looked up at me over the top of his paper. "Any sign of the others?"

"They've been past twice".

"Oh. Didn't they stop?"

I wanted to say, "Yes, of course they stopped, that's why they're standing next to me", but I didn't. It wasn't Nick's fault that Giles and Walt couldn't spot a waving, jumping man exactly where they had arranged to meet him. Short of tying fireworks to my hair and setting light to the hotel, I couldn't think of a way to make us more obvious.

"Do you fancy a cup of tea? Or a pint?"

Nick was reflective. "I'd quite like to get the tents up and have a shower first."

I could see his logic. When you've been active all day, it's all too easy to put your feet up. But sometimes you just have to get those last few jobs done, or they won't get done at all.

Just then, the hire car reappeared and skidded to a halt across the gravel as the driver hit the brakes hard, as if he'd seen the hotel at the last second. Walt and Giles got out.

"Found you".

I assumed they had started some sort of process of elimination, going through all the hotels in Scotland one by one until they eventually found one with me next to it. But they'd found us and that was all that mattered.

We checked in and set up our tents on the little campsite over the other side of the road, using the combination we had been given to open the lock on the wire mesh gate. The ground was dry but soft, and the grass was short. We were the only campers this early in the season. The site was close to the railway line, but the trains were so infrequent that they weren't going to trouble us.

----- x -----

A little later, freshly showered and feeling pleased with ourselves we looked into the hotel for a drink and dinner.

Beers in, we started talking about the ground we'd covered and the journey home next morning, as walkers do.

The only other people in the large bar were four young men at the far end, seated around a table and halfway through their meal.

Nick wandered across to them.

"What do you recommend? What's good on the menu?"

They good-naturedly paused their knives and forks and told him the food was good. Nick checked what dishes they'd ordered and turned to come back to his pint. As he did so the lad nearest him said, *sotto voce,* "Don't have the nachos, they're not very nice."

Nick is a big man, and he's obviously English. It would be hard to miss him in a packed dining room but there was no chance of anyone missing him in an almost empty bar in a tiny Scottish hamlet. And sure enough, Nick's short expedition had been noted. The barman had drunk it all in; without a sound, he suddenly turned and darted from the bar into the back of the hotel.

If you are old enough, you'll remember the Apollo space missions taking off from Cape Kennedy. And you might remember the countdown, *10, 9, 8* and so on, right down to *zero!* At that point, right when you might have expected the rocket to soar up into the sky, nothing happened. Well, nothing obvious happened. In reality, of course, there was lots going on. All systems were go, the engines had fired and were now building up power to thrust the huge rocket into space. At *zero!* there wasn't much to see, but we all knew that something momentous was about to happen.

So it was in the back bar of the Ardlui Hotel. There wasn't anything obvious to see, but everyone knew that something was going to happen.

And then a large man in a chef's uniform came through the door behind the bar, at speed, as if propelled from a gun.

Wiping his hands on a cloth, he cast it to one side, as if to emphasise that he meant business. He made straight for the young men at the far end of the dining room.

Striding to their table, he reached behind himself with one hand and without looking at it, he dragged up a small stool and placed it beneath himself as he sat down. His presence caused the visibly surprised diners to shuffle up the table to make room for him. The chef folded his arms, thrust his elbows forwards onto the table and leaned in, until his face was right in amongst the startled group.

Here, you felt, was a chef with something on his mind.

"RIGHT THEN, LADS." A broad Scots accent that got more menacing as it got quieter. "What's the matter with the nachos?"

----- x -----

Chapter 5
The West Highland Way, Part 2

"How can you explain that you need to know that the trees are still there, and the hills and the sky? Anyone knows they are. How can you say it is time your pulse responded to another rhythm, the rhythm of the day and the season instead of the hour and the minute? No, you cannot explain. So you walk."
Author unknown, from New York Times editorial, "The Walk," 25 October 1967

Months later Nick and I dismounted from the train at Ardlui Station ready to finish business. The station, the hotel and the marina all looked exactly as we'd left it.

We sought out the ferry captain and took the boat back across the loch to the buoy on the pole, where we had left the trail all those months ago.

The weather was even better than last time and we were both in good spirits as we started out. We had been waiting for this moment, using it to sustain us through the dark winter and weeks and weeks of work, and now here we were again. The very detail of the land seemed richer and more distinct than central London. Every pebble, every blade of grass appeared more real and carried a greater presence than the pavements of the city.

As we approached Crianlarich through the woods, we had to make a decision. The trail passes about a kilometre from the town, so walkers have the option of dropping in if they wish, or of keeping going. Nick and I had had enough of towns. We were newly provisioned and back on the trail. The town had nothing we needed but the hills held plenty. We kept on going.

We made some distance and our next priorities became water and a piece of land flat enough to pitch our tents on.

The puddles and pools near the path looked brackish, but eventually I found a larger, clearer pool and filtered some water.

Water is heavy so you don't want to carry it too far. I had brought dehydrated food to save weight; carrying water for any distance would negate that saving. So, having filtered enough water for that evening and breakfast the next day, I wasn't eager to start lugging it around Scotland.

But just a little further on we found a pleasant site to pitch.

We'd made a reasonable distance in good weather, and we'd found water and a good site to camp. But most of all we were back on the trail. First days don't come much better. I enjoyed a Thai chicken meal, sent an abusive text to Giles and Walt, and settled down for the night.

----- x -----

The next day started with a bright morning. There had been a shower in the night but the rain had finished before we got up. The sun came out and we could see the peaks of the mountains around us, between the treetops. I wore shorts as I cooked my breakfast and it wasn't long before we were off again. I couldn't help noticing that yesterday's spring was definitely still in our step.

The path left the woods and crossed some fields occupied by Highland cattle. Ahead of us were two other backpackers, travelling more slowly than us, so we gradually caught them up.

They were two Scots lads. One, a big fellow wearing a red nylon cagoule with no shirt underneath and yellow nylon waterproof overtrousers with no trousers underneath (to save weight, he told us), was perspiring heavily. His mate, a thin chain smoker, was more conventionally attired.

Both were carrying huge rucksacks, and the bigger of the two had a cast iron frying pan about the same size as a helicopter landing pad strapped to the back of his pack.

Both were sociable and they caught us back up when we stopped for coffee later that morning. The big lad in the brightly coloured nylon dumped his rucksack with a sigh. If he hadn't even brought a shirt and trousers, what was he carrying in that huge backpack? I never did find out.

His mate seemed to regard cigarettes as some sort of cure-all, and to his credit, he was keen to share this medical breakthrough.

"Nasty looking blister, mate," shaking open a pack of Benson and Hedges, "Fancy a fag?"

Or, just a short while later, "Headache you say? Try one of these", offering a packet of Lambert and Butler.

By the time we reached the shops in Tyndrum it was so hot that we stopped for ice cream. Nick checked the map and suggested we press on to Bridge of Orchy. Nick likes his showers and he had identified a youth hostel there (with showers) and a choice of pubs.

I couldn't see any of this on the map and just a short while later I found myself standing in Bridge of Orchy reflecting that I couldn't see any of it there either.

We crossed the road to the Bridge of Orchy Hotel. It was too nice to sit inside, so we drank our beer at a table with a sunshade, out by the road. The next table contained an American couple who clearly disapproved of drinking at lunchtime and who made no effort to conceal their distaste. I was reminded of the Raymond Chandler story in which his detective, Philip Marlowe, meets a female client in his office. As she sets out her case she explains that she disapproves of smoking and drinking, to which the laconic Marlowe replies, "Do you mind if I peel an orange?"

Undaunted we sank a couple of pints each and wrecked an unspecified number of bags of crisps and peanuts in the time it took the other couple to drink half a cup of coffee. Then it was packs on, over the eponymous bridge and up the hill.

----- x -----

At the Inveroran Hotel we asked about camping and were directed to a wild campsite (an oxymoron if ever there was one) a few hundred metres further on. We found a flat piece of ground, which had obviously been recently used for camping, tucked away between the bend of a stream and the lane.

A pleasant spot, and it was the work of a moment to get the tents up and to tidy ourselves to the extent required to re-enter civilisation. A little later we were in the bar of the hotel asking about food.

One thing that surprised me repeatedly on this trip was the seeming disinclination of local businesses to capitalise on the thousands of walkers who pass their front doors each and every year. When Nick and I asked for food at the bar we were told, "Sorry, we don't serve food to non-residents". We were quite taken aback. The number of hungry people passing this hotel must be vast, but the management seemed content to self-limit their business to those individuals who had booked rooms. Everyone else who got their wallets out and tried to hand over money were, in effect, politely asked to put it away.

I was all for heading back to the tents and eating my own food, but Nick dug deep into his reserves of diplomacy. The bar staff were actually charming and very helpful, and it turned out that they could offer us food provided we didn't mind having the one dish on offer and on the condition that we didn't mention it to anyone else.

I tried to ask how we were supposed to eat a meal in a busy bar *and* deny it to anyone who asked us about the food, but Nick shushed me and steered me back to our table.

The food, when it arrived, was copious and delicious. Other, later, arrivals looked confused when they asked for the menu and were told there wasn't one.

This strange attitude struck me again as I nipped into the Gents before the return stroll back to the campsite. A sign on the toilet door proudly announced that the toilets were for the use of hotel guests only. So they didn't mind serving me beer, as long as I went somewhere else afterwards to get rid of it.

Back by the bend in the river, we saw that three young Germans had arrived and were in the process of erecting two large tents. From the size of the tents, I first thought they must be part of a much larger party, but when no one else appeared I realised that the three of them were sleeping in two five-person tents. When they packed up next morning I saw that each packed tent was about the same size again as the rucksack each of them was carrying – they just strapped it on the outside. I was staggered that anyone would carry that sort of weight unnecessarily, but it was something we saw again and again. When you've tried it once, lightweight camping is a no-brainer, but for some reason it struggles to gain traction with the great mass of outdoors people.

----- x -----

We had gone to bed in bright sunshine but we woke up in thick fog. I struggled even to see Nick's tent a few yards away. I was up at six, woken by the most persistent, tenacious cuckoo I've ever heard. Two groups of deer watched me with apparent disinterest through the mist as I made tea.

By the time Nick and I moved off, the day had all the makings of a cracker. We followed the old drovers' road and then the military road. An interpretation board told us that this had been the local main road until the 1930s. I tried to envisage 30s-style cars bouncing along it and wondered what the country must have been like when the whole road network looked like this.

The day was going to be a short one, because our next planned overnight stop was at Kingshouse. In the event, we made it easily in time for lunch and our rapid pace led to a debate. Should we camp near the Kingshouse Hotel or walk on? If we camped here, we could get food in the hotel, but obviously not use their facilities (according to yet another sign on the toilet door). If we kept walking we would either have to camp near the A82 main road or press on up the Devil's Staircase (making it a longer day) and camp at the top.

We decided to deal with first things first, and went into the hotel to get some lunch.

The bar was open but completely empty. I asked if we could see the menu.

The barman asked, "Have you booked?"

I felt like I was in a recurring Fawlty Towers nightmare. I glanced around the large, empty bar, and was about to ask, "Why, haven't you got any tables free?" when Nick nudged me gently aside, gave a winning smile and secured us two pints of bitter and a menu.

Again, the first impression was inaccurate and the staff were in reality courteous and helpful. Why they do this is beyond me. We enjoyed the food, paid our bill and decided to press on to the Devil's Staircase.

----- x -----

The switchback path climbing the hill between Kingshouse and Kinlochleven is supposedly the hardest part of the West Highland Way, but in reality it's just a winding path up a mountainside with a cracking view from the top. This beauty seems to have been lost on the British soldiers who built it in 1752: ground down by the fag of carrying road-building materials up and down it, they christened this part of the trail "The Devil's Staircase", and the name stuck.

"Push on up the Devil's Staircase or call it a day when we reach the bottom of it and camp there?"

Nick scanned the map.

"If we go on to the village I'll get some money from the cashpoint. I'll buy the papers and treat you to a nice coffee in the coffee shop while I read them. Then we can push on up the Devil's Staircase. You know I like the papers."

This obsession with reading "the papers" is Nick's only fault, which is a fair indication of what a nice, easy-going guy he is. But when you're spending all day and all night with someone, small issues can assume large size. My memory of lunch the day before yesterday was a mental image of Nick sprawled out on a hillside, half-moon spectacles perched on the end of his nose, his immediate personal space liberally carpeted with broadsheets and colour supplements as he diligently worked his way through *The Independent* and, even more slowly, a large baguette.

Lunch on the hill for me is a shorter, sharper affair, so inevitably I chafe as Nick leafs his way through yet another lifestyle section.

But I had checked the map and I didn't remember any shops at that point, and certainly no settlement big enough to have a cash machine.

Nick handed me the map back and I sneaked a quick look at where we were heading before I pushed it into the side pocket of my rucksack. Nope. Nothing.

We pressed on, the traffic noise from the A road increasing slowly but inexorably as our path neared it.

We walk at different rates, Nick and I. I like to plod on without stopping too much. Nick tends to be a little slower and likes to take the occasional breather. You'd think that would result in problems but it never has. We may split temporarily on the trail, but we always join back up for tea, beer or a destination.

I got to the base of the climb first and took my boots and socks off to give my feet a break. Nick wasn't even in sight so I had a look around me and started a bar of chocolate.

No village. No cashpoint. No coffee shop, in fact no shop of any sort. Just a lay-by and a small house, boarded up and empty.

I guzzled some water and Nick arrived as I was in the stream filtering more. I glanced over my shoulder at him.

"Mine's a cappuccino, mate."

Nick looked around him. "I thought there'd be more here." His tone seemed hurt, as if he suspected some sort of skulduggery on the part of the locals, as if they had deliberately moved the village just to be unhelpful.

He passed me a water bottle and I started filling it.

We were joined by a young Swiss lad. Pleasant enough but not as well equipped as he might have been. In Fort William he'd picked up a postcard with a cartoon map on it and that was his only navigational tool. Nick offered him some freshly filtered water and he started as if we'd offered him heroin. He plainly thought we were mad to drink water from a stream. Not mad enough to be out here without a map and a compass, old boy. I dropped a purifying tablet into each bottle of filtered water and handed Nick's back to him.

Nick and I steeled ourselves and set off up Major Caulfeild's military road. A few drops of rain fell on us, strangely out of a clear blue sky.

As the gradient increased, I reminded myself that Caulfeild's men had carried heavy loads up this hill. Wearing 18th century clothes and 18th century boots, fed on an 18th century diet. So how difficult could it be?

Not too difficult as it turned out. My advice, if you ever climb the Devil's Staircase, is to set a pace you're comfortable with and keep on plodding. Nick's advice, obviously, would be to stop for a breather at frequent intervals. Which just goes to show that when we think we have something worked out, we've really only worked it out for ourselves. One size does not fit all.

I fully expected to leave Nick behind. I anticipated getting to the top well before him, maybe I'd take in the views on this beautiful day, take a few photos and boil some water for a drink.

I assumed the soldiers who built this road must also have used pack animals. If men and animals could carry heavy loads up and down this hill, it couldn't be too hard. My mind wandered to what life here must have been like before the military roads, how much more insular and more local life must have been. These roads might have been built to facilitate troop movements and thereby frustrate any further attempts at Jacobite rebellion, but they must have been the making of the economy in these parts.

Even so, life must have been hard. You could only have bought what had been grown or produced locally; there simply wasn't the scope to send large quantities of consumer goods long distances. And your social circle must have been similarly limited and local.

The gradient steepened a touch and I shaved a little off my speed. In my peripheral vision I became aware of Nick setting an unusually good pace behind me.

What happened there? Nick was much closer than I expected - I should be a long way in front of him. I must have been moving much slower than I thought. I don't usually slow down *that* much going uphill. Too much daydreaming. I stepped out so as to restore the proper order of things, just catching occasional half-glimpses of Nick off to one side or the other as I did so. He was keeping up with me. Just. I kept expecting to see him stop to get his breath but he kept on coming, in complete contravention of his usual walking policy. Fair play to him: whatever he was on, it was working.

We're good friends, no real rivalry between us, but I simply could not permit Nick to get to the top of the Staircase ahead of me. I ignored the sweat streaming down my face and lengthened my stride. But despite my increased effort, the distance between us didn't change much.

I kept at it. The path levelled out and I was there. Turn right and a quick 50 metres to the cairn. Rucksack down and suck in the air. Revel in the views.

Nick appeared behind me. Only it wasn't Nick, it was a tall chap we'd chatted to earlier that morning, back near Kingshouse.

He gave me a smile and a wave. "You set quite a pace, don't you? Your mate's on the slow side, though."

I hadn't been dragging my feet coming up the Devil's Staircase. I'd accelerated to increase an already acceptable pace just because I hadn't looked more closely at the shape behind me on the edges of my vision. My competitiveness meant that Nick was left struggling up the hill with no encouragement from me; indeed, he couldn't even see me. I thought of him sweating his way uphill through the switchbacks and I felt contrite. And defensive for Nick. Who did this bloke think he was, criticising my walking companion?

But I couldn't begin to explain this to the amicable chap who was trying to make conversation with me, so I did the decent, British thing.

"Lovely day."

"It is beautiful, isn't it?"

The formal necessities complied with, the conversation was up and running, and we swapped accounts of our day's walking.

Nick topped out shortly afterwards, and we drank tea and basked in the view down Glencoe. Walking in the UK inevitably means a lot of walking in mist and rain, so when I am lucky enough to encounter good weather, a top view and a pleasing location, I like to take my time and enjoy them. But Nick had other pleasures in mind, because he'd worked out that there was a campsite with showers 7km further down the trail in Kinlochleven. And, for all I knew, a newsagent's.

Nick tried to entice me with promises of expensive coffee while we watched climbers on the ice wall in Kinlochleven and I tried to persuade him to camp where we were with expansive arm gestures and hyperbole. Neither of us was successful so we parted amicably, Nick heading off for his shower and me setting up my tent for an overnight camp to make the most of the sunshine at the top of the Devil's Staircase.

----- x -----

The next morning was as stunning as I'd hoped. I packed up early and started along the trail to Kinlochleven.

The way went steeply downhill, through a series of never-ending switchbacks that made the thighs and calves burn. Nick must have really wanted that shower to add seven kilometres of this to an already respectable walking day!

I followed the old hydroelectric pipeline down the hill to the town, marvelling at the scale of the waterworks. Kinlochleven was a town dependent on its aluminium smelter from 1909 until the plant closed in 2000. Powered by its own purpose-built hydroelectric system, in its heyday the smelter employed 800 people, but by the 1990s it could not compete with larger, more efficient plants elsewhere and in June 2000, it closed. The town has obviously made great efforts to regenerate itself and seems to have had a good measure of success: it looks a pleasant place to live and the inhabitants don't put up notices warning walkers not to use their facilities.

I met Nick at the campsite near the river and waited while he had a morning shower, to wash off the grime that had accumulated since his last shower, the evening before.

Nick struck camp and we strolled to the old aluminium smelter building, which now houses the ice wall, to watch the climbers while we enjoyed the expensive coffee and the newspapers.

There was an ice wall but no one was on it. And there was no coffee shop or newspapers. We consoled ourselves with instant coffee from a camping stove and Nick redeemed himself by supplying croissants bought from a local shop.

Next followed one of the steepest parts of the West Highland Way, out of Kinlochleven and up a series of steep hairpin bends towards the Mamores.

In brilliant sunshine and some way ahead of Nick, I stopped at an obvious viewpoint for a breather and a swig of water. I plonked myself down and savoured the hot, hazy view back across Kinlochleven. This didn't look or feel like Scotland. It didn't look or feel like anywhere in the UK that I knew of. This felt more like backpacking on some Mediterranean island.

What looked like a seed attached to my leg turned out to be a tick. One of the drawbacks of walking in deer country, I supposed. I grubbed about in my pack and extracted my tick remover. It was the work of an instant to twist the little blighter out of my right calf and squash him.

Nick caught up and we exchanged superlatives about the weather and the views.

At about 250m height, we turned into a big, empty hanging valley and made our way along the track. Fortunately for us it followed the contours, which made the walking a lot easier than it would have been if we'd been going up and down.

We paused for a drink at the ruined farmhouse at Tigh-na-sleubhaich. Although this building looks as if it has been derelict for a very long time, it was vacated as recently as 1980. But it doesn't take much imagination to stand among the stones and work out where the people lived, cooked, etc., or to wonder how they felt as they stepped outside their house in the morning and looked up towards the surrounding peaks.

I began to press on ahead of Nick, because the map showed the end of the West Highland Way to be a mere 12km away and I began to develop a feeling that the end was in sight, even though it wasn't.

Waymarking was good so I was never in any doubt as to whether I was on the correct path or not, but along this stage of the Way, walking through thick forest made it difficult to identify with certainty exactly where on the path I was. And some of the forests had been cleared which meant that the forest boundaries no longer matched those shown on my map.

I will admit that I can get rather obsessive about navigation. When I'm walking, I like to know exactly where I am and where I'm going, and I start to get twitchy if there's any doubt. This might stem from one occasion many years ago when I was navigating a group of friends down from Snowdon summit in thick fog. I tried to make the route finding a collaborative exercise, partly to spread the blame in the event of mistakes and partly because I believed that five heads were better than one. I was wrong on both counts.

Unfortunately, a minor wrong turn resulted in an enforced six mile detour with an awful lot of up and down, and that after an already long day. The walk got worse when I fell into a stream and got soaked from the waist down, a situation my friends used to make their views clear by not helping me out.

I no longer navigate by committee. Trust is dead. Even if someone else has planned the walk I still take a map and compass, and I always know my location, even if that someone else is already navigating.

I regard a map and compass as the minimum necessary, usually supplemented by pacer beads.

The most common map scales in the UK and on the continent are 1:25,000 and 1:50,000. The 1:25,000 maps are heavily promoted as walking maps and they show a good level of detail, including field boundaries which can be a great help. 1:50,000 maps show slightly less detail (and not field boundaries) but, since each one covers a wider area than 1:25,000 maps, you need fewer of them. I find it easier to get an idea of the shape of the land from 1:50,000 maps so where they're available, they're my maps of choice. I keep the sheet I am using in a waterproof map case for protection from the elements, spillages, etc.

The only sensible choice of compass is a baseplate compass. This is because a baseplate compass combines a compass and a protractor – very necessary when you start working with bearings. Lensatic and prismatic compasses look very nice and you can spend a lot of money on them, but for walkers they are nowhere near as quick and convenient to use in the field as a simple baseplate compass.

One of the most basic uses of a compass is to help you orient your map. Just align the "north needle" in the compass with north on the map and your map is now aligned with the terrain in which you are walking. The features of the land around you should coincide with the features marked on your map.

When I'm walking, I have to have my map readily to hand because I check it frequently. At any point, I usually know what I should expect to see over the next 500m or so, and I use this technique even if I am following an obvious path. If the map shows that I'm going to walk out of a wood and under a pylon line then that's what I'll be looking for. If I don't come out of the wood or if there's no pylon line, or if I cross, say, a stream where none is marked, then mental alarm bells start to ring. If I don't see what I expect to see, or if I see something different, then I go immediately back to the map to make sense of it. That way it's difficult to get completely lost: if I do stray from my route, I'm rarely far from my last known position.

When I get tired and wet I'm less inclined to root through my coat pockets or rucksack pockets to find the map, and if it's not in a case, I'll try not to get it out in the rain too often. But it's when I don't check the map often enough that the mistakes start to creep in, so ready access to a weather-protected map is essential to this technique.

Another simple technique is to walk a bearing from your map. To do this:

a) Place the edge of the compass baseplate on the map so that it links the place where you are and the place where you want to be (so that the "direction of travel arrow" points in the direction you want to walk);

b) Keeping the baseplate in place on the map, turn the circular compass housing so that the north arrow points to north on the map (usually at the top). The compass is now set – allow no further movement between the baseplate and the circular compass housing;

c) Remove the compass from the map. Allow the rotating needle to point north. Now turn the compass until the north marker on the rotating bezel coincides with the free-moving magnetic needle. Walk in the direction of travel indicated by the direction of travel arrow.

Pacer beads are useful as a method of measuring distance walked. With experience, you'll get quite good at estimating the distance you've covered, and varying that figure for uphill or downhill walking. Pacer beads offer the reassurance of more exact calculation. They were originally designed by Roman legionaries but they've recently started coming back into vogue. They are light, robust, inexpensive and easy to use.

Pacer beads usually consist of thirteen beads on a piece of string; nine separated from the remaining four by a knot. The nine beads count 100m per bead, the four beads count 1km per bead.

I know that 56 of my double paces equal 100 metres (i.e. I count my left foot hitting the ground 56 times) and each time I reach 56 I move one of the nine beads down the cord and start counting again. When all nine beads are down, I've covered 900m. Another 100m means I've covered 1km. At that point, I'll move one of the four beads down and the nine beads all go back up, ready to count more 100m sections.

In his way it's possible to measure distance accurately up to 5km when visibility is bad or when there are no obvious landmarks, for example at night or in fog or a forest. I've rarely needed to use my pacer beads but when I have, I've been glad of them.

On this trip I was using a strip map, one which showed the West Highland Way as a series of strips, detailing the route itself and just a kilometre or two either side of it, so the further on I went into the forests the greater the degree of estimation I was using to fix my position. The advantage of this type of map is the weight saving: because no superfluous areas are shown, every part of the map is relevant and only one map is needed instead of several. But the downside is that you know little of the geography of the region through which you are walking. The trail and a short distance either side of it represent the known world. Beyond that be dragons and all manner of magick.

As I stepped out of the trees into what was shown on my map as the Nevis Forest I got something of a shock. What should have been a narrow path through a big, dark forest looked for all the world like a First World War battlefield. Trees toppled, blasted and splintered lay across each other at crazy angles, in random piles, all across the valley as far as the eye could see.

I know these trees did not occur naturally here, they were planted expressly for timber production. But walking through devastation on this scale I found it impossible not to be moved. I know that the Forestry Commission and landowners like to talk about "farming" trees and "harvesting" timber, and terms like "felling" and "logging" are out of fashion, but I have walked through similar land management before. I had no doubt that these hillsides would be left disfigured for many years, covered in stumps and broken branches, possibly with the next generation of conifers slotted into place amongst the debris. It was a place I wanted to get out of quickly.

By this point my boots had been uncomfortable for about a day, but now they began to hurt my feet in earnest. The Achilles' tendon in each foot throbbed as I started the downhill switchbacks to Fort William. I had bought the boots especially for this trip, and worn them beforehand to get used to them, but now they were making my life a misery. I hobbled onwards, leaving a note for Nick on a prominent branch to make sure he didn't miss a particularly tricky turning, and made it to the campsite.

The campsite was big, with lots of space for family tents and mobile homes, and I wondered how they would take to two grubby backpackers with little one-person tents. I needn't have worried. The staff and the management couldn't have been more helpful, and just a few minutes later my tent was up, my boots were off and I was spread out on the grass waiting for my water to boil to make tea.

The next morning Nick and I left our kit in our tents and travelled light for the last four kilometres to the end of the West Highland Way. After the last few days, walking with no rucksack and no kit felt very odd. My boots still managed to pain me, but a quick side-trip into a cheapo shoe shop for a new pair of trainers eased the pressure considerably.

Nick and I took pictures of ourselves at the sign indicating the end of the Way and promptly sent them to children and girlfriends, keen to illustrate our momentous achievement to uncaring friends and relatives (or, in the cases of Giles and Walt, purely to gloat).

A couple of large full English breakfasts later (termed "full Scottish" for reasons which, other than local pride and some rather novel sausage, never really became clear) and it was time to head home again.

----- x -----

Chapter 6
The Great Glen Way

"I think that I cannot preserve my health and spirits, unless I spend four hours a day at least - and it is commonly more than that - sauntering through the woods and over the hills and fields, absolutely free from all worldly engagements."

Henry David Thoreau

  Today I got lucky and found a seat on the train to work. My usual commute was subtly different this morning and I felt uplifted because of it. I was dressed in my walking clothes and at my feet was my rucksack containing everything I needed to backpack the Great Glen Way through the Highlands of Scotland. I'd change into work clothes when I got to work, but afterwards it would be back into my walking clothes, rucksack on and up to Scotland on the overnight sleeper.

  We pulled into the next station and more commuters got into the carriage. As the train left the station, one of the passengers who had just boarded set herself down opposite me. I glanced up from my book to see what sort of person had joined me in the forced but unspoken intimacy of the railway carriage. She was a young woman, in her 20s, and immaculately turned out. Her make-up was perfect and obviously the product of a great deal of practice, expense and experience. Her clothes were stylish and coordinated, enticing but not too showy, perfect for whatever office she was on her way to. But the effect seemed forced and despite all her effort and investment, the result looked manufactured rather than pretty, so it was all too easy to return to my book.

I got off the train struggling to reconcile my long-held maxim that one should never criticise someone who makes the effort with bewilderment that a whole industry exists to part women from their money in exchange for products of the most dubious benefit, when they could generate results more efficiently and more cost-effectively if they occasionally used a pair of training shoes.

As I passed the cavernous entrance to Tower Hill Station, I inhaled a gulp of unnaturally warm air, billowing unseen out of the underground network. It reminded me of how the temperature on the tube always feels significantly greater than that up on the surface. I recalled reading newspaper reports of passenger groups demanding air conditioning and the authorities pointing out that air conditioning would cool the trains but would also, in the process, shift the heat into the tunnels and platform areas, making the network as a whole even hotter.

So we have a vast underground network that is uncomfortably hot and, directly above it, hundreds of office blocks, the tenants of which must pay through the nose for their heating. As I strode on through the rain, I pondered the feasibility of filtering that warm air, and then piping it upwards and through the office blocks to heat them. A sort of geothermal system but with the ultimate heat source being people and trains rather than the Earth's core.

I derived a smug satisfaction from solving two problems to everyone's mutual benefit, then glanced up at the wet buildings towering above me, hemming me in on the wet street, and I felt a prisoner in the city. A gust of warm air from a tube station! I know several places where homeless people gather precisely to enjoy a draught of warm, subterranean air from a street-side vent. But how much more valuable is that air when it's free and moving across the high fells? That's the taste of freedom, not some fusty blast from a buried railway. And I was one working day away from it.

----- x -----

Nick and I got away from work as early as we could and headed for Euston Station and the sleeper travelling north. The Great Glen Way had seemed a logical extension of our successful traverse of the West Highland Way, starting as it does at Fort William, the end point of the West Highland Way.

We arrived in Fort William at 9.30 on a grey, drizzly morning, and promptly shovelled down a large cooked breakfast in a supermarket café. By 10am we were off, carbohydrate-loaded and kicking our way through the litter of a nearby council estate.

But the Great Glen Way had more to offer and was keen to show it to us. We soon found ourselves in the more relaxed environment of the towpath alongside the Caledonian Canal, quickly reaching the ascent alongside the flight of large locks known as Neptune's Staircase.

The Caledonian Canal was built in the early 19th century by Thomas Telford, but only a third of it is man-made. While Telford undoubtedly did well on the bits he designed, his real genius was in making the most of the existing geomorphology.

The Great Glen is a huge geological fault, that runs across Scotland from the Atlantic to the North Sea. With the lochs of Loch Lochy, Loch Oich, Loch Ness and Loch Dochfour already lying within the fault, Telford had only to construct some 20 miles of canal to link them together and to connect them with the sea loch of Loch Linhe at the western end, and the Moray Firth at Inverness in the east. The result was a route much safer and shorter than sailing north around Cape Wrath, and the construction work served as an employment scheme for an area badly hit by the Highland Clearances.

But by the time the canal was completed, many years overdue and almost twice over-budget, the need for it was not so great. Ship design had moved on, so many ships were now too big to fit through the canal, and Napoleon had been defeated, removing the main threat to shipping at sea.

By the late 19th century the canal had become a tourist attraction and it's remained so ever since. From the walker's point of view, it's mostly flat or gentle walking, with stunning views all along its length, so it's not too difficult to understand its continuing attraction.

But only a short part of the Great Glen Way is towpath walking: most of it is along forestry tracks above the lochs which lie in the Great Glen.

There are drawbacks to walking along a tourist attraction, but one of the advantages (at least according to my map) was that refreshments were readily available. So it was with some anticipation that we arrived at Gairlochy, anticipation which quickly turned to disappointment when we realised the map had let us down. The canal, the mountains and the roads were all in the right places, at least as far as I could tell, but there were no refreshments to be had at Gairlochy.

We crossed the swing bridge and followed the path onto the other bank of the canal, with me craning my neck to catch a glimpse of the pepper pot lighthouse, built to guide ships from Loch Lochy into the Caledonian Canal.

----- x -----

As Nick and I made our way through the woods north of Gairlochy, I noticed what looked like an item of child's clothing by the side of the path and I called Nick back.

I glanced to my right and couldn't suppress a slight shock. A tree was liberally decorated with children's wellington boots. My first impression was of something deeply wrong. It looked like the collection of a deranged trophy hunter, flaunted within clear view of the path.

As I looked further, I could see all manner of tat decorating trees and tree stumps. A phalanx of garden gnomes surrounded one tree, managing to look both benign and threatening at the same time. Benign because they were after all garden gnomes, scions of twee, elderly, working-class garden respectability, and threatening because they were so obviously out of place here, in a deserted wood miles from anywhere.

I stepped cautiously forward, past lanterns and diamante gewgaws, the density of tat increasing as I moved forwards into it. Faint music lured me on. All the time I felt a strange mental dissonance, because the feeling, the impression, amounted to much more than the sum of the junk surrounding me.

Plastic flowers, artificial ponds and the sort of small pottery ornaments that are only obtainable as prizes from fairgrounds. Plastic rabbits and stone ducks watched me impassively as I passed, drawn onwards by the need to ascertain the source of the faint music in the distance, the need to solve this riddle.

I felt like a wandering knight in an Arthurian legend, not knowing what I was entering or what peril was about to enfold me, but drawn ever onwards all the same.

The further into the wood I went, the bigger the "installation" became. If it was art.

I speculated on whether the author was mad or merely artistic, thinking as I did so that there are years of debate to be had on just that subject in respect of almost any artist you care to name. So it didn't take me much further forward in deciphering what lay around me.

Every time my mind decided reassuringly that I was crossing a rubbish heap, I found myself disconcerted by obvious signs of organisation and thought.

I still couldn't escape the feeling that I was in an Arthurian legend, drawn on towards an enchantress. There was no evidence, but I felt strongly that the creator of what surrounded me was female and I was intrigued that someone unknown could create such a strong overall impression with such a total lack of supporting evidence. I looked for reason but I found none. I, the most unromantic and straightforward of persons, needed to meet her and find out what my quest was. And do you know, I was quite confident I could have fulfilled it.

What could be threatening or sinister about a spread of children's toys and fairground tat? Clearly nothing. And yet it was both.

Nick joined me and looked around. I couldn't resist:

"How do you feel about camping here then, mate?"

"I don't think so. There's a strange feeling to this place."

And he was right. How do you transform a wood using kids' shoes and childish tat? Transform it so strongly, moreover, that you change the atmosphere completely, so that even seasoned outdoor people are too uncomfortable to stay there for long, never mind camp overnight?

I left Nick and moved further into the wood, drawn on by the tinkling of music, feeling like Odysseus near the Sirens.

The source of the music was a large set of wind chimes, suspended from a metal bar between two trees and arranged so that their sound carried across almost all of this side of the wood.

I walked out of it still undecided whether it was a fairy wood or a pile of tat. But I guess that's the central dilemma of art through the ages.

As we walked on, into reassuringly normal woodland, a thought occurred to me.

"Do you know, I never once looked up in that wood? Did you?"

"No."

"There could have been anything over our heads. More tat, high up in the trees, or even the person who put all that together, sitting there watching us."

We kept walking, the feeling of the fairy wood fading as we gained distance from it. What more primitive generations would have called its spell, was fading.

----- x -----

As we walked along a lane just above Loch Lochy, towards the hamlet of Bunarkaig, there was a patch of concrete in the grass to my right. From a distance, it looked as if someone had recently demolished a small garage, leaving behind only the concrete base. The concrete shape was hexagonal, which quickly demolished the demolished garage theory. I saw an information board next to it and wandered over to take a look while Nick took a breather.

The board told me that the concrete shape in the soil used to be the base of a replica landing craft, or "Landing Craft; Assault (LCA)" to give it its full military title. Between 1942 and 1945 over 25,000 Army and Royal Marine Commandos trained in this area, and this was one of a number of mock landing craft built for the Commandos to practice their disembarkation drills. Walls of wood and canvas were erected onto the concrete base, and a pit was dug and filled with water directly in front of the landing craft's front ramp, to simulate a beach landing. Training was carried out under live fire to make it as realistic as possible.

I stood there and tried to imagine what it must have felt like on such a landing craft, waiting for the front ramp to drop. What would you expect to see waiting for you? Or would you be so busy carrying out your part of the disembarkation drill that there was no time to look around? What must those men have felt as they leapt into cold water, chest deep, in heavy boots and uniforms, weighed down with kit and under fire?

And that was just the training. The actual landings must have been a thousand times worse.

Most of them, of course, weren't professional soldiers: they came from the factories and the farms, the offices and the mills. I became increasingly conscious of a great debt, and I felt very grateful that so many of them had sacrificed their tomorrows for my today. If the need arose again, would I step up as they did? I certainly hoped that I would. But it's relatively easy to put oneself forward. I asked myself how I would feel if my children were called upon to put themselves into danger to protect the freedom of future generations. The thought made me shudder and I didn't dwell on it for too long.

----- x -----

Unable to find a good spot away from the forestry track, Nick and I pitched our tents on the track verge. Only one vehicle passed in the night and they didn't stop to trouble us.

The next morning we were up at first light and on our way through an overcast morning to Laggan Locks. These two locks connect Loch Lochy with the narrow strip of canal that links it to Loch Oich. There follows a longer length of canal from the far end of Loch Oich to the village of Fort Augustus and then the big one: Loch Ness.

My map promised refreshments at Laggan Locks but again the cartographer was over-optimistic. There was a boat moored nearby, which apparently functioned as a pub in "the season", but it would not open for another month and we couldn't wait that long. So while I made some coffee, Nick demonstrated that he really does have more front than Harrod's by persuading complete strangers to let him into their home and, more importantly, their lavatory.

By now the sky had cleared and I drank my coffee in the sunshine. I watched the house that contained Nick, fully expecting to see people climbing out of the windows, rubbing their eyes and coughing, but Nick re-joined me without incident.

The weather was glorious, and as we followed the towpath the shade of the woods alongside the canal felt very welcome.

At Cullochy Lock, my map showed a toilet block. Useful for getting tidied up before we hit civilisation in the form of Fort Augustus, and as a supply of water, so I was quite looking forward to using it. I suppose that when you've been away from home for a time, simple pleasures can mean a lot.

Unfortunately the toilet block had long since been demolished, leaving only the lock-keeper's cottage.

The cottage was locked and empty, but as I stood in front of it mentally composing a stiff letter to the map publishers about the accuracy of their product, I realised I could hear the sound of water gushing. At the back, a spout of water was jetting out from a pipe high on the side of the building. It must have been spouting for quite a while because it had eroded a hole in the earth at the point where it hit the ground.

I tried all the doors on the off chance I might be able to get in and turn it off, but the place was locked up and while something waterworks-based was clearly amiss, it didn't seem to be serious enough to justify causing damage to get inside.

Back on the towpath, Nick had found a bench in the sun and was chatting with an amiable man who was out emptying his dog. When I mentioned the water leak, our new acquaintance promptly produced his mobile phone and rang the waterways authority. Released by the man's actions from responsibility to do anything more about the leak, Nick and I were free to make our way into Fort Augustus, caught in the throes of its canoe festival, to find a campsite.

----- x -----

The next day dawned warm and sunny, and became increasingly hot. We were gaining height now, and getting dramatic views across Loch Ness.

Loch Ness is big. It's the biggest Scottish loch by volume and the second biggest by surface area. It's also deep, and it's said to contain more fresh water than all the lakes in England and Wales combined.

But despite the weather and the scenery, we were not making quite the same pace this morning as we had done up to now. This fitted my Theory of the Third Day, so I wasn't surprised.

The Theory of the Third Day states that, on any long-distance walking trip, the walking on the first day will be easy, the walking on the second day will be hard (with a feeling that it couldn't get any worse) and then on the third day it does get worse. The rest of the trip will be fine.

In an ideal world, we would start small and build up the mileage gradually over the first few days. However, both Nick and I work for our living and days off are precious, and so must be maximised (that's one reason why we find the sleeper train such an attractive option: we can do our travelling at night instead of using up leave just to travel). The result is that we start as we mean to go on but, inevitably, we pay the price for that in the first days of the trip.

So it was with feet starting to drag, but still gratefully, that I approached the Glenmoriston Arms in Invermoiston.

At this stage Nick was lagging behind, so I thought it would be a nice move to buy some beer and have it waiting for him. But I didn't want him to stick with the main road and walk straight past the pub, unaware that I was inside it. There were some chairs and tables outside the pub, so I settled there with a view the length of the main street. Eventually I saw Nick come into that view, way back in the distance. I waved, he acknowledged. Satisfied that I wasn't going to lose him, I took a look inside.

I made my way through dark wood panelling, across smart red carpets, to the bar, trying not to look like a dirty hiker. The time was a couple of minutes past midday, well within "permitted hours" under the Licensing Act, but the barmaid told me she couldn't serve me alcohol or food until 1pm. Puzzled, I tried to negotiate beer without food; just on the off chance that they might have had problems in the kitchen, but the response was the same. As politely as I could, I asked why it was impossible to get lunch in a hotel at lunchtime.

"Because we don't serve drinks or food until one", was all she offered, but I had to admit her logic had held up to cross-examination.

I felt mildly disconsolate at my failure to secure lunch, but also glad that I hadn't wanted anything more important, like a room for the night. I wandered back onto the small terrace and waited for Nick to join me. We sat at the tables outside the hotel and pondered the peculiarities of Scottish hospitality, and service industries in general. Then I noticed a corner shop just over the road from us and I had a brainwave.

The shop staff were less picky and quickly sold me cans of beer and packets of crisps. I filled a carrier bag and took them back to Nick who had, by now, spread himself out across adjoining chairs and tables and was engrossed in a large broadsheet newspaper, browsing its component parts with a pensive look on his face.

"Do you think we ought to keep these cans out of view? After all we didn't buy them here."

Nick glanced up from his paper and considered the issue for a couple of seconds.

"Well, if they'd like to sell me some of their own beer I'll happily buy it. In fact I'll go further; I'll give them a cast iron guarantee that I'll buy some, if they ever decide to put any of it on sale."

We whiled away the next hour in the sunshine, chatting, drinking and looking through the newspaper, until the official Hour of Luncheon arrived, duly appointed by the guardians of morals for Invermoiston.

The food was good and the pub's terrace was a nice spot, so it was with some reluctance that we set off again into the unseasonable heat.

That evening it took us a long time to find somewhere suitable to camp.

Campsite selection is not usually too difficult. Anywhere reasonably sheltered, flat enough to lie down on and soft enough to get the tent pegs into will suffice. With the common sense proviso that you're not likely to get flooded in the night, or have rocks or branches drop onto you, etc., etc. But a soft, flat bit, big enough for both of us was surprisingly difficult to find.

About the only place that looked big enough and flat enough was the ditch. (After this trip I read an account of a walk along the Great Glen Way in which the writer, similarly frustrated, lay down and slept in what he called a "person-wide depression", which he'd found alongside the forestry track. He woke up with his clothes and his sleeping bag soaked because he'd gone to sleep in a ditch. It had been dry when he got into it but it was very wet after a short shower in the night. One of life's great injustices: to go to sleep in a person-wide depression only to wake up in a ditch.)

It did occur to me that this might have been why they'd been able to introduce a law in Scotland permitting wild camping: the landowners probably just shrugged their shoulders, secure in the knowledge that there was hardly anywhere in the whole country flat enough for a man to lie down.

After many sets of uphill and downhill switchbacks on the path, and lots of detours to check likely sites, we seemed no closer to finding our camp for the night. We were dirty and sweaty, and we were getting tired and fed up. The track crossed a bridge over a steep waterfall and only a few metres further on it broadened out into a space just big enough for two small tents. If the occupants of those tent didn't mind being a bit pally.

It was the work of a moment to put the tents up and start preparing the evening meal, enjoyed al fresco in the warmth and light of a beautiful summer's evening, made even more enjoyable by the fact that summer was still many months away. Loch Ness lay smooth and still, 300m below us, the water's surface just visible through the trees.

The night was warm, too warm to sleep in a thick down sleeping bag, so I spent the first half of it lying on top of my bag.

Next morning I treated myself to a filter coffee while I was still in my sleeping bag. Suitably refreshed I started thinking about breakfast and what the weather might be doing, so I unzipped the tent and folded back the tent flap. As I did so I realised that it was a lot warmer inside my tent than it was outside, and the cooler air flooded into the tent, prompting me to get up.

At this point, it's probably apposite to touch on an important outdoor craft and I'll try to do so as delicately as I can. I refer, of course, to that rarely discussed skill, the ability to defecate outdoors. I've walked with people to whom this is a complete anathema, which is surprising because, a) it's easy and convenient, and, b) it's what humans have done throughout most of our history. And yet some people become the architects of their own misery by contorting their journey around infrequent pub toilets and closed public conveniences rather than simply nipping behind a bush for a few minutes.

There are probably lots of reasons why so many people feel uncomfortable doing this. There's the risk of being surprised or overlooked by other people, the feeling of vulnerability and the likelihood of an accident to name just a few. All of these are relatively modern concerns and they're easily addressed by using a simple system. Becoming proficient at this basic skill will give you much more freedom on your journey.

There are lots of ways we can do it. My way is just one of many, but it's easy and straightforward and I offer it as such.

You will need a toilet kit. A toilet kit consists of:

- A roll of toilet paper (don't bring the whole roll, just enough for your trip),
- A few polythene sandwich bags stuffed into the cardboard tube of the toilet roll,
- A disposable lighter or waterproof matches, also stuffed into the toilet roll tube, and,

- A light trowel or tent peg (if you are unable to scrape a hole in the ground with your boot).

Keep this lot in a small drybag or poly bag, because you don't want it getting wet.

OK, we've got the kit, we've got the urge, what's the procedure? Well, it goes something like this:

1. Select a suitable site. (Use some common sense: make sure you're not going to contaminate a water source, avoid areas of high footfall, etc., etc.)
2. Scrape a hole in the ground.
3. Drop your trousers and underpants.
4. Squat down over the scrape. At this point, you may want to pull your trousers and underwear forwards to improve target acquisition and avoid any friendly fire incidents.
5. Deposit waste.
6. Stand and step away from the target area. This is to avoid you blundering into it while you're distracted by wiping.
7. Wipe. As you do so, deposit the soiled toilet paper into one of the polythene sandwich bags
8. Trousers up.
9. Scrape soil over the waste deposit.
10. Use the lighter or matches to burn the sandwich bag containing the soiled toilet paper. Don't let it set light to anything else and keep an eye on it until it is completely extinguished.

That's really all there is to it.

----- x -----

A little further on we came to a gate, and as we got closer to the gate, we could see a notice attached to it. The notice read:

Caution!
Hazardous Tree
Pass with care

The current mania seems to be to put a notice on everything, pointing out every possible danger, as if that absolves the notice-poster from liability. But even in litigation-mad, health-and-safety obsessed Britain I had never seen anything like this before. A hazardous *tree*? Just how hazardous could a tree be?

At this point let me set my stall out, lay my cards on the table, so to speak. I did realise the full gravity of the situation: even in the days of the Raj in India, when man-eating tigers were on the loose, no one went so far as to put up notices. When the allied forces hit the Normandy beaches there were no warning signs to tell them it might be hazardous. Because someone had gone to the trouble of putting up a notice, it was clear that very serious danger lurked just beyond the gate.

But my intention was to walk along that track. What hazards could a tree present? And without information detailing the precise nature of the hazards posed by this particular rogue tree, exactly what care should I take? I didn't want to appear in the national press as an idiot walker who couldn't take the basic precautions. You know the sort of thing, "Another walker dies - police advise walkers to be properly prepared", etc., etc.

To start with, how was I expected to differentiate this tree from all the others?

I paused to consider the options. What was it going to do? Fall on me? Lure me underneath it and fall on me? Sneak up behind me and fall on me?

I paused nervously and sniffed the air. None of the trees further up the track *looked* hazardous. But obviously, whichever of them was the bastard tree was even more hazardous for not looking so. Cunningly concealing itself as an ordinary tree, it was lying in wait for us.

I decided that there was only one way to take this, and that was on the chin. Cometh the hour, cometh the man, and all that. There was no need for both Nick and I to enter the killing zone, so I tightened my rucksack straps, opened the gate and stepped forward into danger.

Nothing.

I brought up my walking poles, metal tips out in front of me, holding them as if they were a rifle and bayonet.

Still nothing. The silence was staring to unnerve me.

I circled on the spot with my "bayonet" up, and shouted:

"Come on then, you bastard! Let's have you!"

Nothing. The only sounds were a light breeze through the hedgerow and some birdsong. The tree was biding its time, still indistinguishable from its neighbours, waiting for the best moment to launch its attack.

"Come on! Do you want some?"

I can only conclude that my bravery, combined with the sheer force of my presence that day, made the tree think twice, for Nick and I were able to walk up the track unmolested. At least, Nick walked; I zigzagged at speed in case of attack.

As we exited the danger zone I shouted, "Pussy!" over my shoulder, but the hazardous tree refused to rise to my bait. It might have been only a tree, but it knew enough not to show itself.

In Lewiston we stopped for what I can only describe as a fantastic pub lunch and Nick, as is his wont, promptly disappeared into a shop and came back out with a sheaf of newspapers. They all proclaimed this to be the hottest March ever.

As we walked, I noticed that most of the streams shown on my map had dried up completely. And this in Scotland, a country normally wetter than an otter's pocket. I started to think ahead, trying to plan where we might find water with any degree of certainty, pondering as I did so the irony of being unable to find water in Scotland. Imagine trekking around Saudi Arabia and not being able to find any sand, and you'll have an idea of how I felt. Five of the next six streams we passed were dry.

As the path turned away from Loch Ness and took us up onto moorland, at last we encountered a stream with enough water in it for us to dip our water bottles and refill them.

Next was the daily chore of looking for a flat bit of Scotland to sleep on. Today we had to keep on going for an extra 5km, which took us into Abriachan Forest, before we could find somewhere to camp.

----- x -----

The next morning my gas stove was struggling in the cold early-morning air, but once the sun came up it shone strongly, and when the time came to move off I found the bright sunshine had almost dried my tent.

Every Day above a New Horizon

Just a mile up the track was a rather new-age-ish café where we sat outdoors amongst the chickens, while the proprietors brought us coffee and toast. One of the chickens sneaked up on Nick and tried to make off with one of his fingers, presumably to match it with the arm and the leg we'd been charged for the toast and coffee. A textbook example of the aphorism that a thing is only worth what someone is willing to pay for it: there was no other fresh coffee or toast for miles and miles so we paid up without a murmur.

Back on the trail, we started to encounter cyclists, and soon we found ourselves looking down on a city that could only be Inverness, with the sea in the shape of the Moray Firth shimmering behind it.

As we made our way down from the hill with the city laid out in front of us, I found myself pondering the model devised by Ernest Burgess to explain the structure of urban areas.

Burgess published his model in 1924 in the USA. He proposed a model of concentric rings to explain urban land use, starting with the central business district in the centre and moving outwards through a factory zone, a transition zone, a working class zone, a residential zone and a commuter zone.

In 1965, the Burgess model was modified by Mann, a British geographer, to reflect particular aspects of British towns and cities such as the prevailing westerly wind that carries airborne pollution from west to east. Over time, this has resulted in the western sides of cities being less polluted and thus more desirable, and the eastern sides being more polluted and thus relatively less desirable.

But neither Burgess nor Mann included two of the most prevalent land use zones found on the peripheries of almost all British urban settlements. I refer, of course, to the Garden Waste Zone and the Dog Shit Zone.

As you walk towards any settlement, the first sign of human habitation that you notice will usually be dog waste. This represents the maximum distance that the local dog emptiers can be bothered to walk away from the houses before they shake the dog's lead and say, "Come on then", at which point the dog will complete the object of the exercise. A minority of the local dog enthusiasts even go so far as to bag their dog's waste and hang it from the branches of trees or hedgerows, but I'm unable to shed any light on why they do this. Maybe they believe the Poo Fairies will spirit it away in the night. I shudder to think what their Christmas trees must look like.

Just beyond the sporadic dog mess, you will usually encounter piles of garden waste that have been pitched, "Over the back fence". Almost immediately after this, we're moving between gardens and then the first houses. I'll examine where dogging and fly-tipping fit in when the research grant comes through.

So it wasn't long before Nick and I had to be careful where we trod, and I realised that were on the outskirts of Inverness. A quick flash of garden waste and before we knew it we were making our way through lower-middle class post-1918 housing and heading for the central business district.

----- x -----

Chapter 7
The East Highland Way

"After a day's walk everything has twice its usual value."
George Macauley Trevelyan

I looked at my mum across the hospital bed. She looked frail but she had improved a lot since yesterday and it was quite possible they'd let her go home soon.

I hadn't planned to be here. I'd planned to walk the East Highland Way with Nick. It had been his idea; I'd never heard of it and I'm still not sure how Nick discovered it.

We had planned it with our usual cooperative precision. I'd got the maps, checked the route, worked out a likely itinerary based on our past walking pace and calculated our food needs; Nick had roused himself almost to the point where he was ready to find some stuff to throw into a rucksack. I suppose we each prepare according to our needs: I do lots of planning, Nick turns up and wings it, but it works for us. And we had managed to set dates and book the train tickets.

Then the specialist came back with the date for my mum's operation and, for me at least, the East Highland Way was on hold.

The elderly lady in the next bed was listening intently to the young doctor, who was evidently explaining something to her in some depth.

I asked my mum how she was getting on and she gave me a short progress report on herself, and then a much longer one covering the health problems of all the other patients on her ward.

The doctor at the next bed moved on to another patient.

I told my mum what I'd been doing, but there wasn't much of interest to report since yesterday.

The lady in the next bed started a shouted conversation with a woman on the other side of the ward. From the volume, I assumed they must both be hard of hearing.

"DID YOU HEAR WHAT SHE SAID? CALLS HERSELF A DOCTOR? I'VE NEVER HEARD ANYTHING LIKE IT. SHE SAID I CAN'T GO HOME UNTIL I'VE BEEN SICK."

It felt a bit like living next door to an airport runway.

The reply was instant and at a similar volume.

"NO, SHE DIDN'T. SHE SAID YOU CAN'T GO HOME UNTIL YOU CAN WALK WITH A STICK."

I sighed and looked back at my mum. Hard of hearing herself, she'd missed the verbal exchange but she had noticed my interest. As if it explained everything, she nodded towards the other two and said quietly, "Of course, they've both got one leg shorter than the other."

While I was immersed in the idiosyncrasies of the National Health Service, Nick was stepping out on his first solo backpacking trip. I'd prevailed upon him to go without me: it would be difficult to set new dates that suited both of us and it made no sense for him to lose the money he'd spent on rail tickets. I'd had the occasional text message informing me of bad weather and hard walking, but he was doing it. He was out there, doing it.

And just a few weeks later, I was too.

----- x -----

I took the train north from Euston, seated in the "quiet zone" next to an African man who was concentrating hard on a large, glossy book about Nigerian cinema. For most of the journey, he took a succession of calls on his three mobile phones, shouting into each of them that he was travelling to a Scottish university to give a lecture about Nigerian film production. His lunch consisted of an apple and an orange, but every time he moved the book, they both rolled off it onto the floor and under one of the seats, quickly followed by one or more of his mobile phones as he bent forward to retrieve the fruit.

By Rugby, a man sitting at the other end of the carriage felt the time was right to come over and explain the "quiet zone" concept. As he returned to his seat he glanced reprovingly at me, as if say, "You're sitting next to him, that was your responsibility", but his intervention had merely made the cinematographer nervous. After their conversation, whenever one of his mobile phones rang, he became positively frenzied in his attempts to get it out and answer it before the ringing could upset anyone further.

I started work on *The Times* crossword, jolted occasionally by the convulsive, galvanised movements on the seat next to me which inevitably followed the first few notes of the Nokia tune, then nudged and elbowed as the fruit retrieval ritual got underway. By the time we reached Glasgow I needed to stretch my legs and I was glad of the walk to Queen Street Station.

It's easy to forget just how big the UK really is. I had spent most of the day travelling, I was in Scotland and I felt I should be almost "there". But "there" was Fort William, and Fort William was still another four hours away by train.

At Queen Street, I boarded the train north and from my seat by the window, I watched a walker getting on. He was encumbered by a very large rucksack and as he turned, I noticed that his sleeping bag and tent were tied to the outside of his pack. With his two biggest items of kit not even inside his rucksack he must, I reasoned, be carrying a colossal amount of food in there. I wondered what route he would be walking, what wilderness he would traverse, with no opportunity to re-supply. Eventually he worked out that the only place big enough to accommodate his rucksack was the seat next to him, and he sat down with a sigh and got out his reading material for the journey.

He was reading the guidebook to the Cape Wrath Trail.

The Cape Wrath Trail is Britain's toughest trail, 200 miles across Scotland through remote, uninhabited, midge-infested swamps and mountains. That would be why he was carrying so much food! My own trek from Fort William to Aviemore seemed puny by comparison.

I was distracted by a lady who was struggling to lift her case into the overhead rack. It was the work of a moment to offer and then to stow it for her. She sat opposite me and my fate for the next four hours was set, happily, as it turned out.

She was Jill, a Liverpudlian who had holidayed in the Highlands and fallen in love with them. She'd moved there at the first opportunity and had never looked back. She was a mine of information and I was quite sorry to see her leave when the train stopped at her station.

Seeing that I was now on my own, the walker with the huge rucksack nodded at my pack and spoke.

"I see you're a bit better at packing than I am. Where are you walking?"

I told him I was backpacking the East Highland Way, I anticipated four or five days to complete it. He puzzled me by asking how I could "get away" with such a small pack for five days. Surely he'd know all about lightweight backpacking? After all, he was doing the Cape Wrath Trail.

But no. It turned out that he was just here for a weekend, walking with some friends. The guidebook for the Cape Wrath Trail was travel reading only. I was staggered by the amount of kit he thought he needed for a weekend, and even more so when he stood up to leave and picked up two carrier bags in each hand, in addition to his pack.

But my own plans were more pressing.

My original plan had been to walk out of Fort William in the dark, find a suitable spot and camp for the night. But as the train rattled through the Highlands I started to revise it.

The hills looked dark and damp and desolate. Night was drawing in and the only places that weren't steeply sloped were big, black bogs. Jill had pointed out some deer and I'd watched them run away from the train, puzzled how they could do so without sinking in. I remembered too that Nick had experienced difficulty finding the path when he left Fort William and that had been in daylight.

So as the train pulled in to the station I decided to find a hostel or a hotel for the night.

----- x -----

The next morning found me on my way out of Fort William, navigating carefully in the rain.

I passed a grass verge with a piece of new rope lying on it, in which had been tied a perfect hangman's noose. As I looked at it, I pondered the prevalence of lynch mobs in the Highlands, but the rain soon brought me back to more mundane concerns.

I found the point where my path left the road, and as I set off into the woods, I gave myself a mental pat on the back for going into brick for the night. I seriously doubted that I would have found the path in the dark and I was not surprised that Nick had missed it completely.

The skies were grey, the rain unceasing and the old military road to Spean Bridge was wet and depressing. Water lay across the path in big puddles or swirled around and over it in rushing streams.

By the time I reached Monessie, the sun was out and I paused to chat with a farmer on a quad bike. She told me that Scotland had experienced its driest winter and driest spring for years. I glanced at my still-wet jacket and at the ankle deep mud covering the path. I wondered if she had lived on her own in the middle of nowhere for too long. Maybe the years started to blend into one another, the whole lot mixing in with what she'd seen on television. Then I remembered a newspaper report from just a couple of weeks ago that had detailed a bushfire north of Fort William. Three square miles of mountainside went up in flames. More evidence of Scotland's Mediterranean climate: try setting light to Wales with a box of matches in April and see how far you get.

It seemed that the unusually dry weather was causing problems for farmers (I know, show me anything that *doesn't* cause problems for farmers) because it had inhibited grass growth. I wiped the rain off my face and nodded. It was the lambing season and without sufficient grass in the fields, farmers were finding they had to buy feed for their sheep and lambs. This lady had large plastic sacks of it on her quad bike and was driving around the countryside doling it out to enthusiastic sheep.

Hill farming is not a job I would want to do and I wondered how on earth she managed to scratch a living from working so hard to rear so few animals in such harsh conditions. When I passed her house a little further on, I could see that she didn't make a living. The small cottage could easily have been mistaken for a ruin, with its bad roof and rotten doors and window frames. It stood in a small tangled garden, which itself formed an island in a sea of mud dotted with the occasional derelict Land Rover.

I squelched past, pondering what life must be like in such a place.

When I reached the more picturesque ruins at Achnacochine the rain was still holding off, so I paused for afternoon tea.

I reached for the map to check the next stage of my route, but as soon as I'd unfolded it I was surrounded by sheep and lambs, all staring fixedly at me in an assertive manner that I wouldn't usually associate with sheep. Some of them were actually trembling with intensity as they goggled away at me. I don't think I've ever been the subject of such all-consuming admiration from any animal and it was quite unnerving, almost surreal, to experience it from so many, particularly as they were sheep.

I refolded the plastic map case and the whole flock started quivering. Then I realised what was attracting them. I unfolded the top of my rucksack and that set them all aquiver again.

The unusually dry winter had inhibited the spring grass growth and the sheep had become used to being fed by hand. From their point of view, anything that sounded a bit like a plastic sack of sheep food being opened was extremely attractive. For some of them just the sight of a person would cause them to rush across their field, expecting food.

I shooed them away but they would only ever back off for a few feet and even then they wouldn't take their eyes off me, not even for a second. One or two even started edging closer.

I swore at them and they stared straight back.

There is always something a little pathetic about unrequited love, and I'd finished my tea, so I quickly packed and moved on, my fifty or sixty new friends bobbing along, hard on my heels like rats following the Pied Piper of Hamelin.

I shook them off by climbing a gate and pressed on along the path, the plaintive baa-ing gradually getting fainter behind me.

Further on I passed Inverlair Lodge. There are all sorts of stories about Inverlair, some of which are unlikely and some of which are, well, possible.

Hitler's deputy Rudolph Hess is rumoured to have been held there overnight after he parachuted into Scotland in 1941. Several historians have said that this is unlikely, but of course, misinformation as to Hess's whereabouts suited the British government because it would have made an assassination attempt or a recovery mission that much more difficult.

During the Second World War, the house was taken over by the War Office. It was known as "Number 6 Special Workshop School" and one theory is that it was used by the Special Operations Executive to intern their own agents.

The SOE (or "the Ministry of Ungentlemanly Warfare" as it was colloquially known) was the covert body charged by Churchill to "set Europe ablaze". It specialised in espionage, sabotage and reconnaissance, and Inverlair Lodge is rumoured to be a place where SOE agents who knew too much could be kept out of circulation. If a mission was cancelled, or an agent changed their mind and refused to go into the field, they couldn't be allowed to remain at liberty because of what they knew. So, the theory goes, Inverlair Lodge held people who had done no wrong but who could not be allowed to go free. The cult 1960s television series, "The Prisoner", is said to be based on it. Interestingly, given Inverlair's SOE designation, the lead character in The Prisoner is also known as "Number 6".

As I passed the house and grounds, it occurred to me that you could keep someone there in relative luxury and it would be very difficult for them to get away. It had taken me all day to walk here from the nearest town, with proper walking gear; I couldn't imagine trying to get any distance wearing a suit and town shoes.

The next morning I awoke in the glen to a dusting of snow. I could see that the snowline on the surrounding hills had crept down significantly during the night. More worrying was the heavy condensation on the inside of my tent. Nothing unusual there, you might say, but I was trying out a new, lightweight, single-skin tent. It was just big enough for me and my kit, and any movement was likely to result in me or my sleeping bag brushing against the tent fabric and getting wet. Despite the driest winter for years, I didn't fancy my chances of drying anything that did get wet, so I was quite keen to keep everything as dry as possible. The tent is designed to be pitched using a trekking pole as a tent pole and the idea is to pitch it high enough to leave a gap all around the edges, so that what the maker calls the "great ventilation" will dry much of the condensation on the inside.

The night before, "great ventilation" had felt more like "bloody draughty", and I had pitched the tent too low in an attempt to keep warm. Without much airflow through the tent, the condensation had built up from my breath. I made a mental note to set my trekking pole a little longer and thus the tent a little higher when I pitched camp again, later that day.

I made my way up to Loch Laggan, wondering how the farms here could make money. Large fields tucked in between the mountains and the lochs, often partly flooded, with one or two animals to a field. The land didn't look as if it would support a greater density of stock, but how could the farmers turn a profit from such low numbers and being so far from their markets?

The trail became a wide track alongside Loch Laggan and most of the trees next to it had been felled (or "harvested", if you're employed in forestry).

I passed islands that, according to my map, once contained ancient dwellings. Most of our knowledge about them stems from what was found there when the water level in Loch Laggan was lowered sixteen feet in 1934, but what is known isn't much. I stood and looked at them, wondering how desperate you would have to be to live on a tiny island in a lake. You might be safer from attack than if you lived on the mainland, but any time you wanted to do anything much, you'd have to get into a boat and paddle to land to do it. I couldn't imagine doing that frequently and staying dry, and I shivered under my expensive waterproof jacket.

A little further on, the path turned away from the loch and I sat on a pile of logs to eat lunch and check my feet.

I finished with just enough time to layer up before the sky darkened and the next wave of rain crashed in. I trudged on for a few miles, feeling physically battered by the rain on my body, especially during the periods when it turned to hail. As I approached the sawmill near Kinloch, the battering stopped and there was a strange silence. What had been hitting me hard as rain now floated down gently as snow.

It was early afternoon but the dark skies gave an impression of impending night. I walked out of the woods onto the low-lying ground near the River Pattack and the snow turned to rain again. The tarmac under my feet was covered by a couple of inches of water and I sploshed my way disconsolately up to the A road.

Today was turning into a high mileage day and my feet felt on fire. Morale was starting to dip. I considered setting up camp but I wasn't confident I could stay dry in my minimalist tent *and* carry out the various tasks, such as cooking, etc., that I needed to.

The rain eased slightly as I was passing a bench, so I sat down to check my feet again. It was dry enough to check my mobile phone too, and I discovered a barrage of texts from Nick, encouraging me on. To the west, I could see more dark rain clouds speeding my way. Nick urged me on to the village of Laggan; he had stopped overnight in a hotel there and he recommended it heartily.

Buoyed up by the thought of being warm and dry, by hot food and decent beer, I scanned my map carefully to ensure that I was on course for this nirvana. "Carefully" because the bad weather and my tiredness were starting to affect me: I had already made some slight navigational mistakes that I'd had to correct. Now I needed to go left at a T-junction then right at a road fork and look for a pylon line. Provided my current position was accurate.

I set off again and the rain intensified.

I reached a T-junction and a sign. Laggan should be the nearest village but it wasn't one of the options on the sign. I knew I didn't want the place signed to my left, so I turned right.

After a short distance, I paused and forced myself to think this through. I was walking towards a place that I didn't know solely because I didn't want to go to the only signed alternative. But there were an infinite number of places I didn't want to go to. It was folly to assume that walking away from one of them would put me on the right course.

I didn't want to move my aching feet back over the ground I'd just covered from the junction, I'd rather press on than re-trace my steps, possibly in the wrong direction but at least gently downhill and with the rain on my back.

I knew this was not the way to navigate. Comfort is not necessarily a good indicator of direction. I took a deep breath and slopped back through the puddles and the mud to the signpost, and tugged my waterproof map case out of my side pocket once more. I had to hold it at a slant to stop the rain from ponding on it.

In this state or in these conditions (I wasn't sure which), it was increasingly likely that I would make mistakes. So I knew I needed to check and re-check every navigational decision I made. I carefully re-evaluated my decision to turn right.

And found I was going in the wrong direction by 180 degrees.

I tucked the map away and started trudging through the darkening afternoon, wet mud slick across the track. I was horrified that I could have got it so wrong, a disquiet that was only slightly mitigated by the fact that my review processes had, in the end, won the day.

Another five hundred metres and there was my fork in the road near a pylon line.

My attention was drawn away from the satisfaction that I knew where I was and where I was going because, even though I wouldn't have thought it likely, the rain got even heavier.

I knew I wasn't far from Laggan and it was just as well: I didn't think I had much left in me.

Four kilometres to go. Nick likes miles, but I usually think in kilometres when I'm walking because the grid on Ordnance Survey maps is drawn with 1km squares and that makes estimating distances easy.

The rain continued and the temperature was dropping rapidly as I pushed on along the lane beside the river, now threatening to burst its banks. Most of the tarmac was under water and I was glad I had bought new boots for this trip.

The lane seemed to go on forever into the gloom. I half-remembered Fanny Robin dragging herself to the workhouse in *Far from the Madding Crowd*. Fanny broke down her ordeal into its smallest possible components and concentrated on moving herself just one pace at a time. I started doing the same - concentrate on the next step and let the journey take care of itself.

The lane turned away from the river and started climbing a slight hill, towards a farm. Through the murk I could see the lights of the farmhouse and it looked warm and secure. As I got closer, I could see that it was a rural slum and my envy evaporated.

Another 50m and I felt water seeping down my buttocks and legs as my waterproof trousers gave up the unequal contest against the rain. I hurriedly moved my wallet to a drier spot so that my money and credit cards wouldn't dissolve.

I could see the edge of what should be Laggan ahead of me. The rain suddenly eased and I stumped stiff-legged towards the first few houses and the 30mph speed limit signs. I was within striking distance of the village and thus Nick's hotel, and it felt good.

A few minutes later, I stopped at the main road junction in the centre of the tiny village, but there was no sign of any hotel. I checked my map again. The only hotel was almost 2km the other side of Laggan. There was nothing for it; I had to go on.

I now found myself in the gutter of an A road, in appalling weather, stepping out doggedly towards the promised land, while trying hard not to get run over by speeding traffic.

I could see a large house in the distance, set back from the road. It was further than I would have liked but there was nothing I could do about that. I steeled myself by thoughts of shelter. Would I shower first and then go to the restaurant? Or should I eat first and then wash? It might be sensible to check what time they finished serving food and then decide on a course of action. I felt my feet throbbing. Maybe I should devote some time to caring for them? And then there's the bar. I imagined settling down in a warm bar, washed and with a full stomach, enjoying the warmth with a few beers. Or maybe a nice malt whisky? That would be a difficult decision: I'd expect a choice of decent malts up here, so the range of beers on offer would probably be the deciding factor.

The hotel seemed as far away as ever. I know from painful experience that if I neglect my feet when they are painful then they will exact a terrible revenge, so it might be wise to check the restaurant's hours of business and then repair my feet before doing anything else.

I experienced a sudden surge of joy as I realised that the hotel *was* getting nearer, but just a split second after that revelation I was able to see across a dip in the land and I knew that it wasn't. What I'd thought was the hotel was a large private house. The hotel was further up the hill.

But Nick's fulsome praise for the establishment, combined with my own glorious mental images of it, spurred me on and just a few minutes later, I was standing in the reception area of the hotel.

The lobby was quiet and there was no one behind the small counter. When the door clicked shut behind me, the storm outside became hardly audible and I could immediately understand why Nick had recommended the place.

A notice informed guests that the reception desk was not staffed and directed them to the bar. I slipped off my rucksack and took off my coat and gloves.

The bar was empty. I called, "Hello?", and a thin, elderly man came through a door and stood behind the bar.

I asked for a single room.

He looked me up and down, very pointedly, starting at my head and working slowly down to my feet and then slowly back up again.

He told me it was a single room I'd be wanting and he'd have a look but he didn't think they had any, and he disappeared back through the door behind the bar.

The thought that the place might be full, in midweek and out of season, had never occurred to me. And I started to think that it probably hadn't occurred to him either, until he'd decided he didn't like the look of me.

After a decent interval, he reappeared behind the bar to tell me he was sorry but they had no single rooms free.

I said I'd take a double or a twin, but before I'd even finished the sentence I knew what the response would be.

He didn't even check this time, "No, we've nothing".

He went on to tell me about a bunkhouse in Laggan that, "might be more your sort of thing". I ignored the obvious provocation and asked him where it was. I was suspicious because I'd walked through Laggan and I hadn't seen any bunkhouse. If I had, I would probably have fallen gratefully into it.

It turned out the bunkhouse was five kilometres back the way I'd come and some way off my route.

I did a quick mental calculation. If I took his advice I'd have to walk an extra ten kilometres (roughly six miles in old money) just to stand in the same spot tomorrow morning. What a ridiculous idea. If I had to continue walking tonight, it would be towards my destination, not away from it. I thanked him for his help and walked back through to the lobby.

I was fuming as I put my coat and gloves back on, and I wondered what the penalty was for assaulting a hotelier. When I related this story to Giles much later, his solution was both simple and elegant: "I'd have put my tent up in reception and then asked him to have another look to see if he had any rooms free".

I was still angry as I swung my rucksack on and stepped back out into the storm. I was partly angry with myself, because I couldn't help feeling that I had failed to succeed. I'm a clean, well-organised person, respectful of other people's property, but obviously I had failed to communicate that to the man behind the bar. And he was perfectly within his rights to discriminate against me if he wished to. That set me thinking about how it feels to be on the receiving end of discrimination.

I shrugged off the negative thoughts and started thinking about possible sites for wild camping. I crossed the road to investigate a small clump of trees but any camp there would be visible to people in the few houses nearby.

There was a large flat field below the trees so I walked down to see if I could find a private spot, out of the wind and not likely to flood in the night. As soon as I stepped through the gate into the field, I was surrounded by hungry sheep, baa-ing and goggling at me. Within a few seconds, every single sheep in the field was at my feet, the ones at the back pushing the ones at the front nearer to me, like schoolchildren crowding around a playground fight. I couldn't communicate that I had nothing for them and they were obviously diehard optimists. Come to think of it, I doubted they had ever in their short lives seen a person enter their field who *didn't* start dishing out food.

I sighed. I've camped with sheep on many occasions and we've co-existed without incident. They do their thing and I do mine. But I'd get no peace in this field.

A little further along the road, I saw a sign that gladdened my heart. "Bed and breakfast", it said, "Up the hill, fourth turning on the left". Even more importantly, the word "vacancies" featured prominently, on its own little sign underneath.

A further 10 minutes on sore feet brought me to a large house with a bed and breakfast sign in the front garden. It was clearly closed up for the winter and just to dispel any lingering doubts the owners had fixed a large "no vacancies" sign outside. I cursed the idiots who ran the place, who seemed to think that everyone drives everywhere. It had never occurred to them that someone with sore feet, at the end of a long and exhausting day, might regard it as an imposition to walk up a hill only to find the place closed and then have to walk back down it again. Why the hell advertise vacancies down on the main road when they were closed?

I pushed on past Cluny Castle and at long last I found a flat piece of ground, suitable for my camp.

Although I'd had a long and trying day, my situation wasn't at all bad. But if it had got markedly worse I'd have used "the Rule of 3s" to prioritise my next steps. Survival experts teach the Rule of 3s to help their students prioritise appropriately in a survival situation. Although the Rule of 3s sounds specific, it's really only a guide. The Rule states that humans can survive:

- 3 minutes without oxygen;
- 3 hours without shelter in extreme environments;
- 3 days without water; and,
- 3 weeks without food.

Most commercially available survival kits, like the sort sold in camping shops, contain things like snare wire and fishing kit. But think for a moment about the places where you go walking. If a difficult situation forced you to stay there longer than you wanted, how likely is it that you'd start catching fish and snaring rabbits?

In that type of situation, in most places in the UK and Europe, we can take oxygen as a given, and we should be found or have extricated ourselves in three weeks. So The Rule of 3s tells us that our main priorities should be, a) shelter (including warmth and fire), and b) water.

A few minutes later my tent was up (this time pitched higher for more airflow and less condensation) and I was in my sleeping bag. It was late and I was too tired to cook so I ate some sweets, drank some water and settled down for the night.

----- x -----

The higher tent pitch worked spectacularly well and the next morning found me warm, dry and hungry. I checked my map and itinerary – by my calculation I'd covered 50 kilometres yesterday, about 31 miles. At this rate I'd be in Aviemore way too early to use my pre-booked rail ticket. Like Goethe, I decided to burn that bridge when I came to it, and I struck camp.

By mid-morning, I was wolfing down a large cooked breakfast in a café in Newtonmore and feeling like a new man. A short time afterwards I passed Ruthven Barracks, like the military road a relic of the Jacobite risings, and followed the path into a bird reserve.

At the entrance to the reserve was a large group of ramblers, all "of a certain age". They all wore ridiculously stout boots, the men sporting large bushy beards and the ladies wearing resigned expressions, as if they didn't have anything better to do now that the children had left home.

The weather had dried up and, possibly because of my hotel fiasco the day before, I felt that I owed myself a night in brick. Nick sent me the phone number for a B&B and I booked myself in with the charming Helen at Feshiebridge.

Despite the weather, or perhaps because of it, I had made much better progress than I'd planned and at this rate, the next day would be my last.

The land had changed as I'd progressed along the East Highland Way and my final day was no exception. The miles slipped by easily as I strolled through Rothiemurchus Forest, meeting the occasional group of walkers or mountain bikers out from Aviemore. I reached the railway station with plenty of time to catch a series of trains that would ultimately deposit me just a 15-minute walk from my home. I had to pay to vary my ticket and the fee cost more than the ticket itself had done, but I felt it was worth it: I'd done what I came here to do and I wanted to go home.

----- x -----

Every Day above a New Horizon

Part 2

In the Footsteps of Stevenson

Every Day above a New Horizon

Chapter 8
Le Puy-en-Velay

"Don't carry a spare of anything that doesn't rhyme with 'socks'".
Anonymous Internet wisdom on kit selection for backpacking.

My hotel room in Le Puy-en-Velay was clean and modern. It didn't have much character or atmosphere but, I decided, it was functional and it would do. I took quick advantage of the facilities to remove what little grime had accumulated on the TGV.

The scale of what I had taken on loomed before me: 262km across an empty part of France with some camping gear and a bit of pigeon French. I hadn't been allowed to take gas canisters for my camping stove onto the Eurostar, so it was time to test that pigeon French in the big camping store on the edge of town.

I layered up and set off into the rain, a computer-printed A4 street map in my pocket. The weakness involved in exploring with a paper map in heavy rain soon became apparent and I paused to get my bearings by consulting a large municipal street map under a bus shelter.

Le Puy is one of the starting points for the great pilgrimage, the *Camino de Santiago,* and coming down the street towards me, I could see what looked like a cartoon version of a Christian pilgrim. It walked slowly but deliberately, with a stout wooden staff, bent over and holding the ends of a rain cape together against the storm. As the figure got nearer, I saw it was a girl. Like me, she stopped to consult the bus shelter map and we discussed directions.

She quickly dissuaded me from further attempts to buy gas for my stove; unknown to me today was one of the many French public holidays - regardless of what information was on the store's website, it would be closed.

Olivia, for that was her name, was just finishing the *Chemin de Stevenson.* She had walked it, as she described it, "The wrong way", which is to say she'd started walking from my destination, Saint-Jean-du-Gard.

Her rain cape was pathetically inadequate and, not for the first time, I was struck by the preference some people have for style over function. I steered her towards a nearby bar and bought her a coffee. We sat outside under an awning so Olivia could smoke the thin roll-up she'd produced, and as we idled and watched cars splashing down the wet streets, I questioned her thoroughly about the *Chemin de Stevenson.*

She told me that there were many, many dogs, and that they "Like to talk a lot". Great. I've never been a "dog person" and I'd considered buying a sonic dog repeller for this trip but hadn't got around to it. I asked how she dealt with them and Olivia nodded towards her stick. I wasn't sure if she meant she used it to beat them back or if she threw it for them to run after. Clearly, I'd need a plan for dogs.

Olivia warned me to be careful while walking through towns and villages. French footpaths are well marked, but confusion can arise when they cross or overlap, and this tends to happen in towns. It would be all too easy to enter town on the right trail and leave it on a completely different one.

We chatted with a few locals in the bar who seemed fascinated by what we were doing. Or fascinated by what Olivia was doing, to be strictly accurate. I excused myself and left her to find the hostel she had booked.

----- x -----

The next day was grey but at least the rain had stopped. I checked out of my hotel and set off once again to buy gas for my stove. It occurred to me that now I really was on my journey. I stopped to consult my map near a traffic roundabout on a dual carriageway and from the other side of the roundabout I could hear what sounded like an immature driver thrashing an old car. The noise got louder. Irritated by this interruption, I looked up from the map. I saw an ancient Renault 5 enter the roundabout from diametrically opposite me. The engine was under high revs and the car was going too fast. As it sailed past me, I could see smoke pouring from underneath it. The driver tried to leave the roundabout at the next exit, but crossed the traffic island dividing the two lanes and hit a van coming the other way. The Renault bounced off the van and hit a car behind it. It still had plenty of momentum and crossed back towards its own lane, hit a third car and came to rest against a road sign on the pavement.

I watched for a few moments to check that no one was hurt and concluded that there were easily enough people present to deal with the aftermath. They didn't need me and my "Allo, Allo" French. As I wandered off towards the camping shop it occurred to me that if the driver had attempted to leave the roundabout just one exit earlier, it would have been my traffic island he would have crossed and me he would have hit. My walk would have ended before it had properly begun, in fact any future walking would probably have ended too.

With that sobering thought, I entered the camping store and saw to my joy that they sold exactly the type of gas canister I needed. I bought two and left the shop calling down blessings upon them, convinced that their women were beautiful and their men noble and brave.

I pressed on through the quiet industrial estate and picked up my path. At last, I was on a *Grand Randonee!* The red and white flashes of the GR430 would take me to Le Monastier, where Stevenson had started his walk.

I could tell, as if I needed reminding, that I was still near a town, because I passed the occasional park bench by the side of the trail. Seated on the second bench I passed were a couple, with a donkey that stood forlornly in front of them. I'd have happily stopped for a chat, but the male half of the equation looked harassed and annoyed. I noticed that they were both carrying sizeable rucksacks, even though they had a donkey. Maybe that accounted for their demeanour. I slowed just enough to exchange bonjours and kept moving.

On his walk through the Cévennes, Stevenson took an array of equipment, much of which would raise eyebrows amongst modern, lightweight backpackers, including a loaded revolver, an egg whisk and the first recorded sleeping bag, which he'd had made to his own specification. His luggage was carried by his donkey, Modestine.

Modestine proved obstinate and difficult and eventually, after taking advice from local people, Stevenson resorted to beating her and then goading her in order to make any sort of forward progress. But before we judge him too harshly let's remember that today most of us encounter animals mainly as pets; Stevenson lived in a world where animals still provided much of the power that drove agriculture and industry. It must be to his credit that RLS never once seems to have realised that a problem containing an obdurate donkey and a loaded revolver is surely a problem that also contains its own solution.

Unlike Stevenson, I was carrying my own kit and food on my back, so weight was much more important to me. What do I mean when I say weight is important? I've spoken with other hikers, and I've watched them unpack and set up camp. I've seen what they carry and I'm as staggered mentally as they are physically. Top athletes at the very edges of our hobby have broken new ground and the backpacking paradigm has changed. But you wouldn't know it on British hills. Or European hills come to that. Instead of teaching them to do it sensibly, we encourage our youth to carry ridiculous amounts of heavy, bombproof gear for a trip as short as one night. From experience within my own family, this "everything but the kitchen sink" approach is encouraged by the Scouts and the Duke of Edinburgh's Award Scheme. In addition to the usual camping kit, kids on a recent DofE weekend trip were required to carry a complete change of clothes, a spare torch and spare batteries, and a survival bag. Dead weight! The irony that their tents and survival bags were carried in the same rucksack, so therefore if one of them lost his tent he also lost his survival bag, was obviously not apparent to those leading the trip.

Incredibly, after expeditions like these, some youngsters do not lose heart and do actually venture back into the hills. But I wonder how many fall by the wayside, put off by the requirement to lug the equivalent of a small gear shop across moor and mountain?

For reasons I'm unable to fathom, the mainstream gear manufacturers and camping shops seem happy to go along with this charade, making and selling products that are far heavier than they need to be.

The weight of your kit is a critical factor in determining your enjoyment when you are backpacking!

Unless you enjoy carrying heavy loads, the ideal backpack is a light one. When a person is already engaged in hard physical endeavour, why would they want to complicate that by carrying unnecessary weight?

So having, I hope, put up a strong case for carrying less weight, how do we achieve it?

With careful thought, it is possible to reduce substantially the weight carried by most backpackers. Lower pack weight is achieved by:

- Carrying fewer items, and/or,
- Selecting items that weigh less.

Let's start by carrying fewer items. "Be prepared" is an excellent motto but how you apply it is most important. Mental preparation weighs a lot less than carrying every gadget from the camping shop "just in case". Better to develop a mental attitude which will keep you out of trouble, and enable you to deal with it when it occurs, rather than tote a collection of expensive tat around "just in case".

If you have a trip looming, start by making your own list of what you will need. Be ruthless and prune it back as much as you are able. Then do a quick internet search and have a look at the gear lists of people who hike long distances. You'll soon see that many people are able to go out for weeks or months with very little in the way of gear. The writer and broadcaster Nicholas Crane, for instance, walked 10,000km across Europe, a journey that took him 18 months. His spare clothing consisted entirely of one pair of socks, which he took because they could double as gloves if required.

As you scrutinise your list, look for multi-purpose items and redundant items. Anything that serves more than one purpose, such as Nick Crane's socks, is especially useful because it makes other items redundant and allows you to toss them out. Generally speaking, the word "spare" should not be in your vocabulary.

Plan your food and water re-supply points to minimise the amount of food and water you have to carry. It's worth remembering that some cash and a credit card always weigh less than food and water!

Now the second strand: selecting items that weigh less. The three items that are usually the heaviest on anyone's list are their rucksack, tent and sleeping bag. A few years ago my rucksack, tent and sleeping bag weighed 9kg (about 19lbs) in total. My current rucksack, tent and sleeping bag weigh 2.4kg (just over 5lbs).

Lighter kit can be more expensive than conventional gear, but it doesn't always have to be. Nowadays it's perfectly possible to find a tent, rucksack and sleeping bag totalling 3kg at a reasonable price. But it can be difficult to find them in outdoor shops and you might need to delve into the internet to make progress. Why the mainstream shops disregard the move to lighter gear remains a mystery. And if you can't find the weight of an item on any of its labels, you know you're in the wrong shop because they haven't grasped that *weight is key.*

Many lightweight backpackers own a pair of kitchen scales that will weigh to the nearest gram, and they keep a spreadsheet listing each item of their kit and its weight. With this, it is possible to examine permutations of your gear suitable for the conditions you expect to encounter and quickly assess the weight of each permutation.

As you work to reduce the weight you're going to carry, consider the relationship between weight carried, walking and camping. A very light pack makes walking easier, because you have less weight on your back, but camping is harder because you have fewer items to keep you warm, dry, fed, etc. Conversely, a heavy pack makes walking much harder, but it also makes camping that much easier because you have more kit to keep you warm, dry and fed.

The unattainable ideal is a rucksack that would weigh nothing but contain everything you need to camp! The real world ideal is a pack that is light enough to be carried with relative comfort while still providing sufficient shelter, insulation and food options, with enough of a buffer to allow you to cope with an emergency.

I've listed the kit I took in Appendix 1. My rucksack weighed 5.8kg before I'd added food or water.

----- x -----

A little further down the track I stopped for coffee and watched a hare skittering along the path I had just vacated. The hare was soon followed by the couple with the donkey, the whole ensemble looking more cheerful this time. I asked how they were getting on with Modestine, nodding towards the donkey as I did so. This drew the immediate response, "Are you Scottish?" That's probably not a mistake you'd want to invert (if you don't believe me try asking a Scotsman if he's English), but they were French, from Paris, and knew no better.

They weren't the only people I would meet walking with a donkey and I had to admire their pluck. If you haven't read Stevenson's book, or if you have no knowledge of donkeys, you might assume that a long walk would be much easier with a beast of burden to carry your luggage for you. But all you're really getting for your hire money is an extra piece of luggage, a large and temperamental piece of luggage moreover. No thank you, I'll carry my own stuff.

Le Monastier was closed for its afternoon siesta so I was unable to book into the *gîte d'étape*[3] and secure a place to camp in its garden. I walked down the hill to the river and found myself a secluded spot on the campsite there. The sun was out, the river was rushing by and the world felt good.

The next day was overcast again, spotting with rain as I crossed the low bridge over the river. I passed through the territories of many cuckoos in the course of the morning, and met the donkey duo again in Goudet. They warned me several times about the "very hard" climb ahead of us. I didn't want to go up a steep hill at someone else's pace so, after exchanging pleasantries, I left them behind.

After a steep pull for 30 minutes, I topped out. Not too hard at all! I was in a hamlet called Montagne

---

[3] A *gîte d'étape,* or *gîte* for short, is a hikers' hostel.

and, feeling good about my fitness, I reached for my map to check the correct route out of it. My heart skipped a beat. My hat was in the map pocket but my map wasn't!

I thought quickly. The map, in its waterproof case, had probably become dislodged when I put my hat into the same pocket a short while ago. That was at least one kilometre back, and downhill. It could be long gone by now, and if I walked back I would have to repeat the uphill once more. Could I do without it? The trail was well marked, so I could certainly get to Le Bouchet-Saint-Nicholas, the next village, and probably past there and onto the next map sheet. But I knew I'd need the waterproof case: I didn't want to go into the mountains in the second half of this trip with no weather protection for my maps. In bad weather, they wouldn't last more than a few minutes without the case.

And there was a need for urgency. I was about 900m above sea level and it was windy; if I *had* dropped the map onto the path, it could well have blown away by now. There was no other option. I jogged back a kilometre, rucksack bouncing, all the while trying to work out possible alternatives if I couldn't find the map and map-case, and trying to concentrate on the path and fields around me in case I had dropped it on this lane or down that track.

To my huge relief there was my map case, map safe and sound inside it, lying in the middle of the trail, exactly where I thought I might have dropped it. Relieved, I got my breath back and then retraced my footsteps back up the hill. As I did so I reflected on the lesson I had just learned: don't put more than one valuable, frequent-use item in the same pocket. And check often to ensure everything is where it should be. Tighter personal admin about summed it up.

My original plan was to wild camp near Le Bouchet, but as I got closer to the village, I was bombarded with a succession of new-looking signs advertising the delights of the *Gîte la Retirade.* I quickly succumbed and after what seemed like an age, and included a full tour of the village, the stream of signs brought me to the front door of a modern looking *gîte*. It was closed.

I knew that some places did not like their customers booking in too early, and a sign in the *gîte* listed two telephone numbers for travellers to call to secure access. I rang them both but got nowhere.

An elderly man stepped out of the house next door and, after much of my best French, directed me to an *auberge*[4] on the other side of the village. They, in turn, directed me to another, less well signed, *gîte* where I was able to get half board for the night.

The *gîte* owner nodded at my shirt and asked me if I was cold. By now it was a lovely sunny afternoon, but he was done up like it was the middle of winter. Over the next few weeks I would get used to local people asking me if I was cold, even as I was rubbing in Factor 30 sun cream.

There was a large kitchen range in my new quarters, and it was pumping out heat full blast. I took advantage and washed some clothes, leaving them to dry while I walked back to the *auberge* for dinner.

Le Bouchet contains a carved wooden statue of Stevenson and Modestine. Unfortunately, the carver got Stevenson's name and the date wrong, but if you can see past that, it's quite an inspiring design.

The sun shone throughout most of the walk towards Landos, but the strong wind blew the drizzle some distance from where the rain was actually falling.

---

[4] An *auberge* is an inn, usually with a restaurant.

This created a strange effect, because I was walking in bright sunshine, with a sharp, distinct shadow, in driving rain. I noticed lots of water standing in fields, and running off in clear, full streams. My route was isolated and quiet, and the streams reminded me of something but I couldn't think what.

I went through Landos and on to Pradelles, my destination for the day. Pradelles is a medieval town that looks part well turned out and part decrepit. It's almost as if some people in the town mean well and have put some work into their town to show their civic pride, while a significant minority aren't having any of it.

I had arrived in Pradelles earlier than I'd expected so I had a quick re-think and decided to go on to the next town: Langogne. The track was empty and except for a herd of cows being rounded up by a man with a yapping dog, the countryside seemed quiet. Just before Langogne I met two Australian ladies, walking with carefully printed directions in a plastic sleeve. We exchanged pleasantries and we were to meet many more times before our trips ended.

----- x -----

Chapter 9
Langogne

"All truly great thoughts are conceived by walking."
Frederick Nietzsche

In Langogne, I found a pitch on a campsite by the River Allier, just a short walk from the town centre. My boots weren't as comfortable as they should have been and when I took them off I saw why: the insoles in both boots had collapsed. There was no rebound, no sponginess left at all, under the ball of the foot nor under the heel. Moreover, in each boot the insole had started folding over onto itself. This was a sure route to blisters unless I did something about it, but my chances of finding new insoles in such a small town were as thin as my socks.

I carried out a stocktake of my food and decided I had enough to eat at my tent, without going into the town. This was a bonus, as I didn't like the look of the man in the tent near the toilet block, or his dog, so it meant I could stay with my kit. After the episode with the map, I knew I couldn't afford to lose anything, whether through negligence or theft. Next, I revised my itinerary to even out the distance I would be walking each day. Instead of longer days followed by a rest day, I planned a series of shorter days with no rest day, hoping it would be easier on my feet.

I hadn't brought a charger for my mobile phone because of the extra weight that a charger and plug adapter would cause. So I switched my mobile phone on just long enough to get and send some texts, then offered mental thanks to no one in particular for my girlfriend Debbie, and Giles, Walt and Nick. All were interested and encouraged me onwards.

Next morning I took a leisurely breakfast and chatted with a neighbouring camper who was touring with his wife in what looked like a bizarre midget caravan which, he proudly told me, he had built himself.

The builder of midget caravans told me that the town shops would be closed, "Because it's Monday". By this time I was used to every other day being a public holiday in France, but "Because it's Monday", was a new one on me. I started to wonder why they bothered.

Undeterred, I strode into town to look for insoles. I found a pharmacy, checked the opening times and found that it was due to open soon. The lights were on and I could see someone inside but after a quarter of an hour, when she opened the door to put out some rubbish, she quickly told me that the pharmacy was closed all day. As were most of the shops in town, if I was interested. This was bad news. Langogne was one of the few towns of any size on my route: if I couldn't get what I needed here, I would have problems.

I asked if there was another pharmacy in the town, which would be open, and she directed me back down the main street. A few minutes later I was looking around a very modern chemist's shop, stroking the shop cat and, since I didn't know the French for "insoles", taking one boot off to show the old insole to the elegant lady who worked there. She was too polite to actually grimace, but it was obvious that she understood. She quickly conducted me to large display rack covered in packets of insoles, every one of them too small for my needs. We umm-ed and aah-ed, each in our own language, and then she produced a single pack of American-made insoles. She didn't know if they would be any good?

They were perfect and they saw me all the way to Ales, at this point still 190km away. I thanked her profusely and scurried off with my prize.

Walking footwear is a highly personal thing, even more so than underwear, I would suggest. Socks made of wicking material, which moves moisture away from the foot, are extremely useful because they remove one of the main causes of blisters.

Fit is also critical, but unfortunately shoes and boots that fit in the shop can be most uncomfortable on the trail. Over the years I have come to the conclusion that the only way to be certain a pair of boots fit me well, is to wear them for a hundred miles with a pack on my back. If they're no good, not many places will take them back after that, and in any case, by then I'm a hundred miles from home.

But I've found there are some things you can do to improve your chances of success:

1) Wear wicking socks to help keep your feet dry.
2) Take good care of your feet. That means train to be fit for long-distance walking, keep your toenails trimmed *and* filed, and, when you're out on a walking trip, check your feet every day.

3) Don't take a chance on suspect footwear: if it's not comfortable in the shop, it won't get any better on the hill. Fit is key.
4) Wear your walking socks when you try on boots or shoes. Never rely on the in-house socks loaned by the store.
5) Buy slightly bigger than your usual size. Your feet will expand on a long-distance walk.
6) Buy boots or shoes with PU midsoles, not with EVA midsoles. The midsole is the part of the shoe between the grippy outsole and the removable insole, and its job is to provide cushioning and stability. Anything providing cushioning must "rebound" to its original state, or there is no cushioning effect. In my experience, EVA loses its rebound very quickly, the more so because I'm a fifteen stone man with another stone of kit, food and water on my back. A compressed midsole means that the fit of the boot is different and I've had some very nasty blisters from this phenomenon. PU midsoles last much longer.
7) Go as lightweight as you dare and take some of the weight off your feet.

----- x -----

A short while later I was back on the road, relishing the comfort afforded by different socks and the change of insoles. The sun was beating down and as I walked, I thought about last night's texts and the people who had sent them. I wondered what would be waiting for me on my phone when I turned it on again that evening.

The trail was empty and I couldn't remember the last time I had seen any donkey hoof prints, so maybe my Parisian friends were falling behind.

I reached a granite tor surrounded by trees and there I saw a Swiss man I'd lunched with back in Goudet. We greeted each other and he explained that he was taking photographs of the tor because it was "a special place". He had a female friend who was writing her third book on "magical places" and he knew she would be interested in the tor.

I almost replied, "There's a lot of that new age crap about", but I bit my tongue just in time as I realised that, like his friend, he too was into "magical places". He was a retired teacher, now working as a "youth-oriented lifestyle coach". I come from a nation in the grip of austerity, where people are losing their jobs and their pensions in droves every day, and the idea of a country where people can make money by pumping out pseudo-spiritual books and afford to hire youth-oriented lifestyle coaches fascinated me.

But I was more interested in social history than mumbo-jumbo. I was in an area, which in the eighteenth century, was terrorised by The Beast of Gevaudan. The killings started in 1764 when a peasant woman, Emmet Marden, was killed and partially eaten while tending a flock of sheep near the village of Les Hubacs. Over the next three years, more than a hundred people were killed, usually by having their throats ripped out. Witnesses spoke of a wolf-like creature, the size of a cow, with razor sharp claws and teeth. The beast seemed to prefer women and children, and would even ignore sheep and cattle in the same field in order to attack humans. The French mounted large hunting expeditions and sent soldiers, but the killing continued and the beast got bolder, on one occasion in 1765 attacking and killing several people at a big spring fair.

In September 1767 an exceptionally large wolf was killed, and survivors of earlier attacks identified it as the beast by scars on its body made by victims defending themselves.

But just fifteen months later the killings started again, and it wasn't until 1770 that a second large wolf was shot with two silver bullets (as insurance in case the beast turned out to be a werewolf) and the attacks finally ceased.

As I walked through the forests and fields, I tried to imagine how I would have felt on these same paths in the 1760s. Economic necessity meant that the herds and flocks would still have to be taken out to pasture, and brought back again, beast or no beast. Rather like today in the UK, gun ownership was restricted to a small stratum of society, leaving me wondering how I would have protected my family in the 1760s, and how I'd do so now if the need arose.

I saw no sign of the Beast during my travels, but I know from experience that it's always best to do your thinking before a crisis rather than trying to think in the middle of one, so I carefully formulated my strategy well in advance. What would I do if the Beast showed up? My plan probably reveals more about my nutritional needs on a long walking trip than it does about the practicalities of dealing with large wolves: I decided I'd eat the bastard.

I passed another full stream on the way in to Cheylard l'Eveque and the sight helped me remember what the streams here reminded me of so strongly. Most streams and rivers have some vegetation nearby on the banks, then a strip of mud or gravel and then the water, often murky. But in the painting "Ophelia" by Millais, the vegetation extends right to the water's edge and trails in it, and the water is clear. Just like every stream I'd passed so far, minus the corpse of Ophelia of course.

I was getting hungry as I wandered into Cheylard and my thoughts strayed back to my lunch. I found myself wondering why the French seemed unable to sell a decent ready-made supermarket sandwich. The made-on-the-spot stuff was superb, but every time I browsed the cold cabinet in a shop, I was depressed by what I saw. It was almost as if they simply couldn't be bothered. On the other hand, maybe they didn't value anything that wasn't made in front of them. You want rubbish, they seemed to be saying, we'll give you rubbish. And those piddly little quarter litre glasses of beer, what are they thinking?

----- x -----

I spent the night in a superb *gîte* in Cheylard. Chastened by the temporary loss of my map, the next morning found me checking and double-checking that I'd left nothing behind before setting off under blue skies into the thick morning mist.

As the sun burned off the mist, I sought patches of shade as the path passed through forests of pine and beech. The fields looked green and fertile, and I found the countryside different from Stevenson's description, "one of the most beggarly countries in the world ... like the worst of the Scottish highlands, only worse", particularly as I'd been in the Scottish Highlands only a few weeks before.

I reached the chateau at Luc just after lunchtime and made my way downhill to the deserted campsite, near a waterfall on the river. A sign on the small toilet block told me to camp and then pay at the café in the village when I left.

I ate my lunch and watched small birds flying low and fast, seemingly to leave the area as quickly as they could. Then two large birds of prey arrived and began flying leisurely up and down the River Allier. I suspected they were hunting, and just by luck I had a seat on the halfway line, so I nursed my mug of tea and watched intently. After about ten minutes they were joined by a third bird, to my uninformed eyes identical to the first two, and the whole performance looked a lot more like two males competing for a female. There seemed to be quite a bit of, "What are you looking at?", and, "Do you want some?", but the female stayed aloof; I couldn't detect anything that equated to, "Leave him, he's not worth it".

By evening, the wind had picked up strongly, and before bed I made a few excursions to collect large stones to place on my tent pegs, to ensure they didn't come loose in the night.

The wind kept up all night and by morning it was raining heavily too. Yesterday's clear blue sky had given way to solid grey, the colour of old pewter.

I struck camp quickly and made my way through the driving rain, up to the café, to pay for my use of the campsite. The reaction as I walked in was a bit like in the old western films when the sheriff walks into the saloon: everyone stopped what they were doing and turned to stare at me. "Everyone" being the *patron* and two labourers whose van was parked outside, all of them merrily cocking a snook at the smoking ban. I offered my best "Bonjour" but, without so much as a flicker of acknowledgement, they all turned away from me as one and went back to their conversation. I waited at the far end of the bar, dripping politely.

The conversation finished and the two labourers drank their coffee. The *patron* rearranged some glasses behind the bar, and then seemed to realise that I wasn't going away. He put his towel down and made his way slowly across to me. I said I'd come to pay for the campsite, thinking that the prospect of free money might ginger him up a little, but he merely placed a plastic folder in front of me, with the charges for camping glued to the cover. I paid and left, wondering if anything short of the Spanish Inquisition could get a full sentence out of that lot. As I plodded down the road in the rain, I imagined the head of the Inquisition interviewed on local television, in front of a backdrop of hooks and thumbscrews, "We're not asking anyone to recant or anything, just a civil word…"

I'd kept an eye out for any sign of food or a menu in the café, but they just served coffee and cigarettes, a theme I was to find again and again.

I walked on, gradually uphill. I'm very careful in my selection of walking and camping kit, and sometimes that means I buy something expensive. But the dividend is that when the weather is bad, I can keep it on the other side of my clothes. The inside, where I am, stays dry and at a nice, workable temperature.

That's the theory, anyway. But to my annoyance I found that my boots and overtrousers were both leaking profusely. Not a small leak, which gradually gets bigger, but a complete equipment failure from the waist down. Very quickly, my legs and feet were soaked and the cold wind was starting to chill me. I'd trusted this stuff and it had betrayed my trust. As I trudged on, the unreliability of kit I'd previously thought trustworthy began to unsettle me.

I speeded up in an attempt to generate some body heat and started to think about how I might dry out. The rain seemed omnipresent and overpowering, and it was not going to let up anytime soon. The ideal would be a campsite that evening with a restaurant nearby.

I reached La Bastide-Puylaurent late in the morning and saw a small *supermarché* on the main street. Outside the shop, an attractive young woman was struggling to manoeuvre an uncooperative donkey under the shop's awning and so out of the rain, while two men stood by and watched, oafishly cracking jokes. Eventually the donkey was in the dry and tied to the railing, and the woman joined one of the men, who turned out to be her partner. I concluded she was investing too much time in managing the donkey and not enough in managing her relationship.

Once inside, I found that the shop served coffee and I asked for a *café au lait*, only to be told that they served coffee, not coffee with anything. Put firmly in my place I sat and nursed a thimble-sized cup of black coffee, and wondered if I could drag it out long enough to dry off a little. It didn't really matter, my trousers and boots would still leak the moment I stepped out into the rain once more.

The couple joined me with coffee-thimbles of their own. They had started in Langogne and had six days to travel as far as they could with their hired donkey. They left before me and I bought a few items for lunch.

I quickly caught them up on the edge of town. The girl was wearing a small cape, wholly inadequate for keeping the rain off, and her boyfriend wore a nylon cagoule and denim shorts. He told me he only had one pair of trousers with him and he wanted to keep them dry. We were about to cross a high, bleak part of France and I didn't envy him one little bit. I decided I'd stick with my two layers, albeit that they were soaking wet.

They told me they hadn't booked any accommodation and would just take what they could find, something I found heartening because I knew I might have to think about a few nights in brick if the weather failed to improve, although the need to find donkey-friendly accommodation must have limited their options.

Like most of the cavalry I met, they were moving much more slowly than I was. I added that to my already extensive list of reasons never to hire a donkey, and pressed on up the hill ahead of us, into the cloud and rain. As I did so it occurred to me that their last view of me must have looked like the last sighting of Mallory and Irvine on Everest in 1924, "Going strong for the top", and we all know how that turned out.

I was walking along sandy, earthen tracks, which had turned to mud, edged by short trees and shrubs. The foliage on each side of the track was impenetrable and the cloud swirled about me. I had decided to aim for Chasserades, 12km away.

12km should be achievable, I felt, but despite having all my layers on, I was still cold and this was starting to worry me. The more so since I wasn't sure what I'd find in the way of accommodation in Chasserades.

Despite the rain quickly levelling the sandy soil on the track, I'd started to notice donkey hoof prints which looked quite recent, and I turned a corner to find the Parisian couple with their donkey under a makeshift tarpaulin shelter which was about a quarter of the size they really needed to stay dry. The donkey looked even more forlorn than usual.

They both looked up, surprised to see me and, I felt, with a slightly furtive air, as if they were doing something they didn't want widely known. The woman had her hands down the front of her husband's trousers and I wondered if I'd stumbled across some sort of outdoor sex scenario (which confused me because this really wasn't the weather for it), so I prepared to pass by quickly with a cheery wave. Then I saw that they were trying to rig up a rain skirt for the man, by fashioning a black bin liner around his nether regions.

They kindly offered me a bin liner for myself, but I pointed out that I wasn't from Paris and so fashion wasn't as important to me as it was to them.

Standing still meant getting cold, so I kept moving.

I walked through the village of Chasserades, noting the *chambre d'hôte*[5] as I passed it and waving to the two Australian ladies and a French couple, all sitting comfortably in the conservatory. How I envied them that conservatory! Sitting in the warm and the dry, wet things drying upstairs. I contrasted that image with my squelchy boots, and I used the next two kilometres to compose my complaint to the camping shop after my walk, when I planned to return the boots and get a refund.

My reverie was interrupted by a steep downhill stretch into Mirandol where I decided to stay overnight at the *gîte*. A man in the adjoining house told me to speak with someone who was in the *gîte*, so I made my way round to the front door.

----- x -----

---

[5] *Chambre d'hôte* – bed and breakfast establishment, sometimes offering half board.

Chapter 10
Mirandol and Mont Lozere

"We walked because that is what we did."
   Bill Bryson on the Appalachian Trail

Inside the doorway of the *gîte* was a large dog, fast asleep across the doormat. By virtue of his size and weight (and possibly temperament), he was completely blocking any sort of access. I'm aware of the adage, "Let sleeping dogs lie", and I regard it as sound advice, but I had to nudge the dog aside with the door in order to get in. It felt a bit like handling nitro-glycerine and I was careful to carry out what you might call a dynamic risk assessment as I did so, but the dog just raised one eyelid lazily and lowered his head again. There was a distinct odour of large, wet dog throughout the kitchen area but I wasn't about to kick him out.

Once inside I could hear a shower running. I gave the premises a quick once over and saw that the *gîte* was clean, smart and modern. There were plenty of beds, but only one of them had any kit near it.

The shower stopped and the *gîte's* only other occupant joined me in the kitchen to introduce himself.

He was Olivier, a 40-year-old French agricultural worker from a vineyard near Beziers. His big, smelly dog was called Torc.

Getting cleaned up was good for morale and the opportunity to dry clothes and equipment would give me a head start on the weather tomorrow, I felt. I sipped a cup of tea and checked my messages.

The *épicerie*[6] in Chasserades had been closed when I'd passed it (surprise, surprise) but Olivier told me it would probably be open now, and he had decided to walk back to it. I wasn't about to backtrack a couple of miles just for a baguette, so I suggested he give it a miss, but he was adamant. Did I want anything? I suggested we go halves on a meal and some wine, and I gave him some money.

After an hour or so, Olivier was back and showing me his purchases. He'd bought pasta, bouillon cubes, two types of ham, grated cheese, and some bread, but he'd saved his greatest prize for last. His manner told me that I was in the presence of something significant, and with what I can only describe as genuine reverence, he delicately unwrapped a large sheet of white wrapping paper and summoned me over to take a look. We both peered in at what appeared to be small turd covered in mildew.

Judging by the look on his face my response, "Does it do tricks?" was probably not quite the reaction he'd anticipated. But underneath the mould was goats' cheese and had I but realised it, I was trampling on his dreams.

Later that evening we discussed our families and our aspirations, and I discovered that Olivier's ambition was to get out of viticulture. He wanted a little place of his own and a flock of goats, so that he might produce

---

[6] *Épicerie*: grocery shop.

cheese of the sort that he'd gone out of his way to procure for me. Typical Frenchman: the cottage in the country isn't enough, he has to produce a sought-after cheese as well.

Olivier told me that one branch of his family had emigrated to England during the religious strife which followed the suppression of Protestantism in the 18th century. Maybe I'd heard of them?

I've worked in London for many years and I was used to people who don't live there asking me if I knew so-and-so. I never did. But I knew more about Olivier's family than he did. The family name was Bazalgette, and Joseph Bazalgette, later Sir Joseph, the civil engineer, made such great improvements to public health in London that there is still a memorial to him on Victoria Embankment.

----- x -----

The next day I was out early and moving uphill through beech woods so fresh and green that it was impossible not to feel uplifted simply by being there. The forecast was more rain, but not as much as yesterday. It was threatening when I paused to wander around the deserted village of Serremejan, but still the rain held off. If I'd known what was coming I might have felt a lot less cheerful.

Before long, I met the two Australian ladies I'd passed in Chasserades, when they'd been snug in the conservatory of their bed and breakfast accommodation. They told me that they'd got to their accommodation quite early in the afternoon, and the proprietor put them in the conservatory for three hours while she finished her lunch and prepared their room! They were still seething about it and told me how they envied me my ability to walk a little further if I felt like it, and to vary my itinerary as I pleased.

I laughed and told them how I'd wished I'd had warm, dry accommodation like they had, as I'd squelched past them in my wet trousers and leaky boots.

The campsite in Le Bleymard looked good, but it was early: if I kept going, I could knock off some of the climb up Mont Lozere and have an easier day tomorrow as a result. If I could beat the rain, I'd still be dry when I got to the ski station and I could take my pick of two *gîtes* and a campsite. I could feel that the temperature had dropped. I glanced over my shoulder and saw that bad weather was closing in. All the more reason to get cracking then.

The road signs and street furniture in Le Bleymard carry a profusion of red and white GR flashes. Unfortunately, not all of them show the path number. I remembered Olivia's advice back in Le Puy: be careful where GR paths overlap, especially in towns, but I still spent ten minutes following the wrong route and another ten getting back onto the right one.

I left the town and headed across fields to start my ascent of Mont Lozere. Mont Lozere would be the highest point on my route, 1,699m above sea level. That's not very high as mountains go, and it's not even half the height of the highest mountain in France. But to put it into perspective, the highest point in the UK is Ben Nevis at 1,344m, and most British walkers know how bad conditions can get on the top of Ben Nevis.

I was very close to the place where Stevenson camped, the experience about which he wrote so movingly in, "A Night Among the Pines". The way ahead was a wide earthen track, recently bulldozed smooth and starting to become slick as the rain spotted onto it. I was going to lose the race for shelter before the rain arrived, so I paused to catch my breath and put on my waterproofs. If I could get there before I got soaked, I'd still regard that as good progress.

As I started to leave the forested part of the mountainside, I passed three Frenchmen, all slogging slowly up the hill, wrapped in hooded rain capes that looked increasingly inadequate as the rain intensified. We exchanged greetings as I strode past them. I felt slightly guilty as I did so, because I knew it was possible that there might not be many vacancies at the *gîte* ahead, and I was determined to get one.

I got to a modern ski lodge and entered a smart-looking, empty bar, to check in. I asked the proprietor for a bed for the night and he asked me to wait for a moment.

After ten minutes the three Frenchmen in rain capes came in, shaking the water off their capes and stamping their feet. I was glad I'd got there before them.

But not for the first time I found I was thinking according to my own cultural norms. There would be no orderly queuing here, and I was ignored as the three Frenchmen enquired about the availability of beds and were booked in ahead of me, then each conducted to his room. Finally, it was my turn and I was shown into a small dormitory that contained the two men I'd shared with back in Cheylard. There I'd found them friendly and unobtrusive – ideal traits in a shared bedroom with limited space. Their faces both lit up as I was shown in and it was a good feeling to be so well received. We shook hands and they cleared one of the beds for me.

There was a two-hour wait before dinner was served and we spent it in the bar. You might have thought that six men of similar ages, thrown together in a bar, might break the ice and strike up a little social discourse, but not a bit of it. It quickly became obvious that any attempt to initiate conversation would be stillborn. One hedonist ordered a hot chocolate, and after the ripple caused by such licentious behaviour, we sat there in an unnatural silence. I couldn't help feeling that if we'd been thrown together in an English pub we would have got friendly long before dinner was served. But maybe not: this was about more than just location, it was about culture.

The mood changed completely at the dinner table, the social niceties lubricated not by alcohol but by food and the attendant rituals that seem so important to the French. I quickly discovered that my two roommates (Jean-Pierre and his friend) were prolific walkers with much experience. The other three were two brothers and their friend Michel. Although I know that it's the French version of "Michael", the name "Michel" always sounds like a girl's name to me. And it sat incongruously on this Michel, who must have weighed twenty stone and sported a huge bushy beard. We enjoyed a convivial evening, in complete contrast to the strained atmosphere in the bar earlier on.

I was asked how far I walked each day. I usually make between 20 and 30 kilometres depending on the terrain and on my schedule. I lacked the French to explain that my distance varied each day and, to be honest, I felt that I should have been doing more than I was. I've read accounts of people walking the big American trails and they hit 20 to 30 *miles* each day, sometimes for day after day after day, so I felt rather shame-faced as I handed over my itinerary to illustrate my daily distance. But it was met with murmured conversation and low whistles. They had already seen me push straight past them on the climb to the lodge and my itinerary seemed to confirm their impression that I was some sort of superman.

I quickly realised that, unless you're working under a time restraint, a decent daily distance is whatever you want it to be. In terms of time, some of my new friends spent as long walking each day as I did, but they "only" covered about 10km a day. The more I thought about it the more I realised that I had developed a near obsession with mileage. I was to meet others who shared this more relaxed approach as my journey went on.

That night I slept like a log and when morning came I was in no hurry to get up and face the rain again. Eventually I stirred myself and found that the rain had gone: in its place were a clear blue sky and a cloud inversion in the valley below our dormitory window.

Breakfast was the usual overhyped and undernourished affair. One of my roommates was an elderly chap and I watched as he took his time over two small pieces of bread and jam, and a coffee. I ate exactly five times as much bread as him and then, when he wasn't looking, I sneaked his yoghurt to supplement my own which I'd just finished. We still had some height to make before we reached the summit of Mont Lozere and for the life of me I couldn't see how he was going to make any headway on a couple of scraps of bread and some coffee.

But as I stepped out of the lodge and pulled on my rucksack, I saw him heading up the mountain like a long dog, Jean-Pierre beside him, matching him stride for stride. How he could achieve that on little better than starvation rations I'll never know.

By this time, the clear blue sky and my cloud inversion were long gone, and rain was threatening once again.

A line of ancient *montjoies*, ancient standing stones placed to show the route in bad weather, led me up the hillside. As the undergrowth petered out and gave way to wind-blown grass, I began to develop a reassuring feeling that I'd been here before, even though I knew I hadn't. The higher reaches of the mountain were bleak and barren, but they looked like the Brecon Beacons in south Wales, where I've enjoyed many a night under the stars. I felt as if I was on home turf, reassured by the fact that the Beacons were a known quantity. I knew what to do in this environment. I would be all right.

I was the only person on the peak and I could see bad weather coming in from the north, so I didn't hang about. I might be confident in my abilities, but I didn't want to test them if I didn't have to.

I dropped down across a snowfield and stumbled down a long, crumbly, rocky gully, buoyed up by the knowledge that I'd just knocked off the highest point on my journey. I was soon in the small village of Le Pont-de-Montvert, at 895m above sea level exactly 804m below the peak I'd just crossed.

I found a campsite next door to the Gendarmerie and got my tent up minutes before a torrential downpour started. At that point, the rain was a minor inconvenience and I felt I'd beaten it by putting my tent up before it hit. As I made myself a meal from the remains of yesterday's baguette and ham, I had no idea that the rain I could hear drumming on my shelter was to become a defining feature of my trip.

----- x -----

Chapter 11
Le Pont-de-Montvert

"There is nothing like walking to get the feel of a country. A fine landscape is like a piece of music; it must be taken at the right tempo. Even a bicycle goes too fast."

Paul Scott Mowrer

There was a lull in the rain, but it was obvious that more was coming so I layered up before I went to explore the village. Two large marquees had been erected next to the Gendarmerie and I could see people setting out tables and moving sound equipment. It looked for all the world like a summer wedding reception which was about to be spoiled by the weather. Cosy and dry in my waterproofs, I wandered on in to the village.

Le Pont-de-Montvert, population 290, nestles in a natural bowl surrounded by steep, grassy hills, covered in late May by bright yellow broom. It stands at the confluence of three rivers, the Tarn, the Rieumalet and the Martinet, and the rivers are a powerful defining feature of the little town. Its history is another.

I knew from Stevenson's book that the religious War of the Camisards started here in 1702, some years after the Catholic government of Louis XIV had decided to suppress Protestantism, and the region's Protestants formed themselves into armies to fight back. The area around Le Pont-de-Montvert was the setting for many appalling atrocities, some of which took place in the buildings and streets of the village in which I was now standing. Superficially, it was a pretty little place with its rivers and bridges and old houses, but I knew the town's dirty secret. I knew about the torture and the murders which these old stones had witnessed, the psalms and the visions, and that knowledge tainted everything I saw.

I was roused from my reverie by a man who dashed out of a bar and waved me in. At first, I thought he was a tout and asked him if they served dinner, but to my embarrassment he was the male half of a couple I'd passed on the trail a few days before. They quickly had me seated at their table, drink in hand, as we discussed our homes and families. They were from Brittany and they were good company. Not for the first time I found myself wishing I'd made up a small book of, say, half a dozen photographs showing my children, my house, my job and so on. It would have been a useful aid.

They warned me of the weather forecast and I asked them what eating establishments there were in the village, but they only knew of the inn in which they were staying. Which is how, some 45 minutes later, I found myself sharing a dinner table with the two Australian ladies I'd met a few days before, who were staying in the same inn. We were just discussing what a small world it was when the door opened and Michel and the two brothers from the lodge on Mont Lozere walked in. Unlike everyone else, and by virtue of being a lone walker, I knew every diner in the restaurant.

The weather forecast seemed to be the talk of the evening, and the Australians told me that prolonged heavy rain was on the way. They would be taking a taxi to cover the next day's stage of their walk.

I'm not obsessive about covering every inch of the route, and doing so only on foot, as some walkers are. But I didn't think things would get bad enough to justify motor transport; I thought they probably wanted a break and the weather forecast provided a convenient justification. I did tease them a little but I was too polite to push the point.

After dinner, I strolled back to the campsite, passing the party at the gendarmerie, which was now in full swing. Being nosy and hoping to mump an invitation to the party, I stopped to chat with two young men who were standing outside and holding bottles of lager. They were gendarmes, and the party was being held because one of them had been posted to Guadaloupe. My French wasn't good enough to ascertain if this was regarded as a good posting or a poor one. Since Guadaloupe is a Caribbean island, I'd imagine the former. They were pleasant enough, but I wasn't invited in so I continued to the campsite and made myself comfortable for the night. Unlike Michael on Cherill Down, the gendarmes had been good enough to give me warning of their firework display which took place later that night, so I didn't have to jump about and fumble for my boots when it started.

It must have begun to rain soon after I went to bed, and at about one in the morning I was awoken by the ferocity of the rain hitting the outside of the tent. I checked my shelter from the inside and everything seemed to be holding up against the onslaught.

But a few hours later, I was woken up again, this time by occasional drips of water falling onto my face. I checked again and found that the condensation from my breath had reached such a level that it was dripping from the centre line of the tent, onto my sleeping bag and me. Normally this moisture would have stayed on the inside of the flysheet, but the high wind was pushing the tent flysheet against the inner, wetting it and causing it to drip.

Thunder and lightning boomed and flashed overhead as I considered my options.

It was 6am. I considered getting something absorbent to mop the condensation off the inside of the flysheet, but every article which I might have used, I needed to keep dry. Clearly, as long as I lay there exhaling moist breath, the drips would continue. The rain had been torrential and unrelenting for some five hours and I knew that if the forecast was correct, it would continue for much longer. I could stay and get wet or I could move myself and start getting organised.

I quickly thought it through.

I was planning to walk 27km along high paths to Florac today. It was still early so I had plenty of time. Being stuffed with down and very lightweight, my sleeping bag was the item of my kit which was the most vulnerable to water, so I would get out of the bag, pack it away to keep it as dry as possible, don boots and waterproofs, grab some easy-to-eat food and head for the toilet block to ride out the storm.

A few minutes later, I was standing in the toilet block with my valuables bag, blinking through the rain at the zipped up tent that still contained my things. Bored but dry, I started eating and thinking.

An hour later and I'd eaten everything I'd carried from the tent except my camera and my wallet. The only time I'd seen rain like this was many years ago, in a typhoon in Hong Kong. Even then, the rain had ebbed and flowed. This rain was hard and persistent – it didn't ease up even for a minute.

I still had to recover my kit and strike my tent, but I had a nagging sense of unease at the back of my mind. I tried to concentrate on the here and now. I noticed that the pitch I had selected contained a depression that was starting to fill with water, and the waterline was getting closer and closer to my tent.

By 9 o'clock I'd made two sallies into the deluge and I was back in brick, with my kit, my rucksack and my tent. It was time to confront that nagging sense of unease.

As I watched the weather, the like of which I'd never seen before, I pondered the practicality of my original plan. I'd planned to follow the footpath from the village another 400m up the hillside and then walk the 27km to Florac. But I couldn't even walk into the village without getting soaked. If I couldn't function effectively here, at 895m, how the hell would I make progress at 1300m?

What did I know that I could use as a comparison? As I've already said, I've often walked in the Brecon Beacons, and I know that the highest point there (and the highest point in southern Britain) is Pen-y-Fan, at 886m. When the weather is bad on Pen-y-Fan it can easily become a survival issue: hikers and even soldiers have died there. I was at a similar elevation here, but I still had a lot of height to gain if I was to walk to Florac. For the first time I started to examine the wisdom of my plans. As I stared dismally at the driving rain, it was with a jolt that I realised my thinking was faulty.

I'd thought that my choice was between walking to Florac or getting a taxi there, and my sarky comments to the Australians had left me reluctant to consider a taxi. I'd walked in bad weather before; and anyway, how bad could it be?

But as reality dawned, I knew that wasn't the choice at all. With leaking trousers and leaking boots, and weather bad beyond my experience, my real options were a taxi to Florac or a taxi to the nearest railway station and a train home.

It was a low point. I didn't want to go home: if I did, I'd feel compelled to come back here another time to finish my walk. But as I thought through the mechanics of getting higher up and walking to Florac it became more and more obvious that I could be taking my life into my hands if I walked. Going home was unacceptable and taking a taxi was unpalatable, but those views meant that my thinking kept short-circuiting, causing a light marked "walking" to come on repeatedly in my mind.

I made myself a cup of tea and forced myself to consider the options properly. Sensibly considered, I wasn't going home and walking wasn't an option. So, a taxi it was then.

Once I'd made the decision, and by mature reflection, my frustration evaporated and I started thinking through the next set of problems. Where was I going to get a taxi in a tiny hamlet like this? I'd passed a tourist office, so I could start there, if it was open. Failing that, the inn. They must have had to call taxis for their guests before now.

Just at that moment, a pot-bellied, elderly man, carrying a green plastic washing-up bowl full of dirty crockery and drenched even through his raincoat, jogged into the toilet block. He called out something cheery in French and started filling his bowl with water in one of the large sinks.

He told me the weather was bad.

I choked back the impulse to thank him sarcastically for the information, helped by the lag-time as I considered how you tell someone in French to go and boil their head.

I kept it civil. After all, it wasn't his fault he had a nice dry caravan to live in. So we chatted as far as we were able and I asked him if there were any taxis available in the village.

Yes, it was possible to get a taxi, he told me. Just go to the café and ask them to phone one. *C'est simple.*

I thanked him, shouldered my pack and set off into the storm. I had to go down a lane into the village, across the bridge and just a few metres along the riverside to the café. Most of the fields in the area seemed to be draining themselves down what was formerly the lane, but I managed to pick a course that kept the water from going over the tops of my boots. I passed the inn where I'd eaten last night and was about to turn right from the narrow street onto the little bridge when I saw what, for this sleepy little village, amounted to traffic meltdown.

Two cars travelling in one direction had met one car going the opposite way at one end of the bridge, and now none of them could go anywhere. Highly amused by the concept of gridlock caused by just three cars, I stood grinning, fascinated by the arguing, the gesticulating and the added emphasis provided by the car horns.

Then I noticed that one of the cars was a taxi. Right there, right in front of me! I ran over to it and tapped on the driver's window. Or where the driver's window would have been if the car had been English. Cursing myself for my provincialism I started to make my way round to the other side of the car, but the driver very decently wound down his window and asked what I wanted.

"Êtes-vous libre?"

With a curious logic he explained that yes, he was free, but no, he couldn't take me anywhere.

The other two motorists began shouting their displeasure at the cabbie and I briefly wondered if a fight was about to start, and whether I wanted to be involved if one did.

The taxi driver ignored them with magnificent distain. He had been booked by people in there, he told me, people who wanted to go to Florac, and he pointed at the inn where I'd had dinner last night.

This must be the taxi booked by my Australian friends. I wondered if they'd want to share. It seemed likely: they were both friendly people, and they would save money by splitting the fare with me.

The other two drivers managed to sort out the traffic jam without further involvement from the taxi driver, so he and I made our way to the inn.

The cabbie had indeed been booked to take the two Australians to Florac, but he was also going to carry another couple so his taxi would be full. I asked him if he'd come back and repeat the journey with me and he assured me he would. Then, as if to remind me what a small world we live in, my friends from Brittany appeared and said they'd come with me.

----- x -----

Two hours later, I was in the tourist office in Florac. I'd noticed a supermarket just a little way up the road and I needed some food, but I knew from experience that French facilities and services often seem to function as much for the benefit of those they employ as for those they serve, and I wanted to find a room for the night while the tourist office was still open.

The lady there was most helpful and soon sorted me out with a bed in a nearby *gîte*. She'd heard of Robert Louis Stevenson and she asked me if I was doing the walk with a donkey, as he did. With my halting French, I tried to explain that, no, the walk was difficult enough as it was without building in further complications. She told me that donkeys could be very helpful with the right handling. I remembered Stevenson's comment when he sold Modestine at the end of his journey. He lost money on the animal but in selling her, he reflected, "I had bought freedom into the bargain". I was warmly developing my theme that I couldn't see much use for donkeys in this day and age, beyond feeding cats, when my erstwhile friend told me that she owned many donkeys and ran a business hiring them to walkers.

She didn't ask me if I wanted to hire one.

I left the tourist office buoyed up by the prospect of cooked food and a real bed for the night. As I stepped outside my spirits got a further boost from the rain: at long last it looked like normal rain. It hadn't stopped and blue skies were not going to appear anytime soon, but the torrential downpour had, at least, eased up just a little.

So it was with a bounce in my step that I walked the length of the high street and crossed the car park to the supermarket entrance. I got there just in time, to the second, to watch the manager bolt the doors shut in my face and put up a sign informing would-be shoppers that the store was closed for lunch and would then remain closed for Pentecost.

I've never been quite sure whether I admire the French for running their affairs to benefit employees as well as customers, or whether I think it's socialism gone mad. I tried to remember if I'd passed any small shops that might still be open and as I did so there was a bang of thunder so loud, it made me jump. Almost at once, like a bad horror film, the rain intensified, lashing down onto me, the car park and the closed supermarket.

I turned and ran back to an archway where, trapped by the driving rain, I had time to ponder the vagaries of French public holidays.

I wondered what would happen if a supermarket in my town put up a notice saying that they were closed for Pentecost. I suspect people would be banging on the doors demanding to know who Pentecost was and why they'd shut the shop for him.

When the rain eased enough for me to walk without being physically battered by it, I made my way back to the centre of town. I found a charming little pizzeria and ordered a large pizza.

The food arrived and it was appetising and hot. That alone would have left me well disposed towards the place, but the experience was greatly enhanced by the waitress who was in her 40s and incredibly beautiful.

Stuffed with pizza and dazzled by the unexpected glamour, I staggered back out. I had developed a yearning for something sweet and the beauty of walking long distances is that you can eat pretty much anything you want without putting on fat, so I found a small shop and bought too much chocolate. Then I sheltered under the shop's veranda and ate the lot.

As I did so, I reflected on my day. The course taken by RLS and Modestine to get from Le Pont-de-Monvert to Florac is now a busy main road and the French have re-routed the footpath up along the nearby mountains. Strangely, the unplanned changes to my itinerary had kept me on Stevenson's route, while my original plan would have taken me away from it. I finished the chocolate and wondered if I'd be able to get my boots dry by morning, and what the preliminary signs of trench foot were.

----- x -----

My room was at the other end of town in a 1960s-built study centre that seemed to have all sorts of classes running over the weekend and many mature students in residence. I took my time over a shave and a shower, and then decided to crack on and wash some laundry while everyone else was in class and unlikely to discover me.

A few minutes later and my clothes were drying over a radiator that was pumping out heat full blast. I wrote up my journal and did a stocktake of my food. Heartened by being clean and dry, with laundry done and well placed for food, I made my way down to dinner.

At dinner, I found that I was "Monsieur" (according to the lady in charge) and I was the only person out of about a hundred diners who was given that appellation. I was shown to a table already occupied by two young lads from Normandy. Roman and Tomas were affable, and the only conflict was when we found that I wanted to use them to practice my French, but they saw me as a good opportunity to practice their English. The resulting linguistic crossfire made for a lively evening. They were just setting out on a camping trip, but going in the opposite direction to me. Like me, they'd been forced into brick by the hostile weather.

I mused on the weather for a while. It seemed bizarrely unpredictable from where I was sitting. I mean, if you're outdoors a lot you get used to looking at the sky, checking the wind direction and so on, almost as second nature, and you can generally work out what the weather will do over the next few hours. But here there seemed to be no prevailing wind direction as far as I could tell. That morning I had stood for nearly three hours watching the downpour and its direction had changed every few minutes. I often saw clouds travelling in opposite directions meet and then go off in a new direction. Weather-wise this part of France seemed a swirling pool of conflicting air currents with chaotic *météo*[7] being the result.

Roman and Tomas announced a plan to hit the fleshpots of Florac after dinner and very decently invited me along. They were good company, and I would have liked to extend the evening with them, but I was dog-tired and my only footwear was still wet so I politely declined.

That night I slept like a log, until 4am when I awoke with a start. Something was wrong, but what?

Then I realised I couldn't hear the drumming of heavy rain any more. I scrabbled to the window, drew back the curtains and peered out across the wet tarmac of the car park. Sure enough, after 27 hours of some of the worst rain I'd known, it had stopped. I tried to go back to sleep, but the experience of the last day and night had left its mark and for the next few hours I could only cat nap, mind on full alert for any sound of the rain starting up again.

By 6.30, the rain was still in abeyance. Big black clouds were scudding up from the south, but the lighter clouds behind them seemed to promise a better day. By 7 o'clock, the wind had changed and was gusting from the west, bringing a whole new set of big, black clouds into my day. I sighed. There was no way I could

---

[7] *Météo*: weather.

calculate the weather in these circumstances, I would just have to get on with it.

I walked alongside the River Tarn, roaring and in spate (the river, not me), and crossed it to get into the valley of the Mimente.

I was walking through whole hillsides of chestnut trees, sometimes planted on terraces, sometimes just scattered higgledy-piggledy. There were a few other species, usually invasive types like sycamore and beech, but the chestnut trees were overwhelming. It occurred to me as I walked that the leaves on these trees had just reached their maximum beauty. A few days before and they wouldn't have been fully out; in a few days' time they would lose that initial new leaf freshness. I was seeing them at a point in time that would not be repeated for a whole year.

Annoyingly, for I was lost in my own thoughts, at this point a French walker attached himself to me. He was slightly older than me, dressed mostly in black and he was rather damp. His black rucksack had a fluorescent green rain cover over it, an incongruous splash of colour on an otherwise monochrome man. He'd noticed me checking my map and wanted to look at it. He had no map, and his guidebook was wet and disintegrating.

I'm always keen to help anyone else, especially with something as important as navigation, so I flourished my map again and he took a good look at where we were and where he wanted to be.

Unfortunately, he seemed to interpret this minor kindness as something that created a lifelong bond of friendship between us, and he stuck to me like glue. I didn't want to be rude to him, so there we were, me trying to get back to my thoughts and him pacing alongside me, yammering away and undeterred by my obvious inability to understand him.

I've often found that when people try to communicate with others who don't fully speak their language (and I include the English in this) they tend to fall into one of two camps. If the person they're trying to speak with doesn't understand, some people will speak more slowly, emphasise key words, or even rephrase what they were saying in an attempt to be understood. And then there's the other lot who simply repeat their sentence again and again, without varying the words or the speed of delivery, as if the blunt force of mere repetition will drive their message home, something akin to hammering in a nail. Determined to define themselves by Einstein's definition of madness, they do the same thing over and over again, each time expecting a different outcome.

Sadly for me, my new travelling companion fell into the latter group and he had a lot he wanted to say, so I had to endure the same-sentence technique again and again, until I wanted to take him by the neck and squeeze the very life out of him.

I tried to lose him. I'd wait until the path narrowed to single file and then take a toilet break, or stop to take a photo, only to turn around and find him patiently waiting for me. If he pressed ahead, I'd hang back in the hope that he'd clear off, but he just slowed or stopped until I was level with him again.

The path ran horizontally along the steep hillside and at one point, it curved around to cross a steep-sided little valley that cut across it at right angles. The stream which usually flowed down this channel was swollen by the recent rain, blocking our path completely.

I looked it over. It could be waded and my boots were still wet anyway. There didn't seem much alternative and I'd only just made up my mind when my colleague asked to see my map. Then he outlined his plan, which involved forcing a path through undergrowth for two kilometres up a 45 degree slope, crossing the stream higher up and then forcing a route back down the same slope, through the undergrowth again, back to the path. The man was clearly an idiot and my patience was at an end. I moved him to the side of the path and undid my rucksack's hip belt so I could ditch it more easily if I went over in the water.

"Get out of my way", and I was straight into the stream and out the other side, striding along the path once more.

A few minutes later I heard him behind me, scurrying along to catch up. As the path widened he fell in beside me again, but it was clear that his heart was no longer in it. The incident at the stream constituted a *decree nisi,* which became *absolute* the next time I stopped to take a photograph, and I was on my own again.

----- x -----

The war memorial at the hamlet of Saint-Julien-d'Arpaon seems to carry more names than the village has houses. I wondered if the memorial covered a region rather than a village, of if rural depopulation was the cause of this apparent mismatch. The area was leaking people to the towns and cities when Stevenson passed through and as employment prospects diminish in the countryside and increase in urban areas the process has continued ever since.

Saint-Julien-d'Arpaon was where I joined the Mimente railway.

The old Mimente railway is a lovely walk. The track is long gone but the track bed remains and it makes for pleasant walking. I strolled along it, enjoying the faltering sunshine, but unable to shake the impression that I was being followed as I walked through the old tunnels. The line was built shortly after Stevenson travelled through the area and it closed as long ago as 1948. Not so good for railway enthusiasts but excellent news for walkers, for it provides an even path with gentle gradients, and enough social history to keep things interesting. And I could hear crickets chirping for the first time, my first indicator that I was now in the south!

I arrived at the Gare de Cassagnas and secured myself a bed in the old railway station. I was the only inhabitant in a six berth room, with its own little bathroom and toilet. I took the best bed, piled my stuff on the only chair and hoped I would still have the whole room to myself at bedtime.

Tidied up and sorted out, I left to explore my new surroundings and quickly bumped into the two Australian ladies, Blonwen and Sandra. We chatted for a few minutes and they were amused that I didn't notice anything unusual about Sandra.

I looked her up and down. She seemed well enough. Then I noticed that one of her boots was missing. Her foot was encased in padding and wrapped in a plastic bag. She looked like the victim of some appalling chemical burn accident.

I asked what had happened.

Where I'd shouldered aside a Frenchman and strode into the stream earlier in the day, Bronwen and Sandra had been more reflective. They had reached the same point and paused to give some thought as to how best to cross the water but still remain dry.

Like me, they realised that trying to go around was not an option: there was a steep, densely forested slope above and a gorge below, so they'd decided to wade.

Bronwen took off her boots, tied the laces together to string them around her neck and waded across. She sat down on the opposite side and began the process of drying her feet and re-lacing her boots, and as she did so, she was just in time to watch Sandra's crossing.

Sandra had decided not to hang her boots around her neck as Bronwen had done. To her it seemed all too likely that she would drop them into the stream and be left with wet boots, so she threw them across.

Actually, that's not wholly accurate. She threw the first boot and it landed safely on the other side. But when she threw the second, it struck a branch over the water, dropped into the stream and was swept into the gorge and away, all in less time than it takes to tell.

For a moment the two women had stared, dumbfounded, at the point where they'd last seen Sandra's boot. They realised the difficulty of their position: two women in their sixties with 12 kilometres of rough mountain path to walk, and only three boots between them. But they seem to have treated the whole thing as a bit of a lark. They quickly fashioned a makeshift shoe using a foam sit-mat and some bandages from their First Aid kit, then taped a plastic bag over the top to keep the water out. Then they walked the 12 kilometres of mountainside. They were still giggling like a pair of schoolgirls as they recounted the story for me.

That evening at dinner, they had to retell it a number of times and I found it impossible not to be impressed by their positive attitude.

----- x -----

Bedtime saw me sharing what was formerly my room with four other people. Everyone was very considerate of others and very discreet, and before long, we all settled down for the night.

By six o'clock the next morning, I was awake and trying to still a very burbly tummy. Around the edges of the blinds, I could see that outside the sun was up and getting on with the day. Inside the bedroom, I could hear occasional movements and the odd muttered comment, and I knew that I wasn't the only person awake; like me, most of the others were wondering whether to snatch another half hour in bed or whether to rise and shine.

As if to influence my thinking, my stomach gave a big lurch, and it occurred to me that I'd better get into the bathroom before the others because I knew I'd struggle if I had to wait my turn in a queue. In fact, any sort of waiting was out of the question: I'd better get moving straightaway.

The bedroom was still in darkness so I got up carefully and quietly, and felt my way to the toilet. I made it without dropping or knocking anything, or disturbing the tranquillity of the dorm. The toilet walls were paper-thin and I could even hear the hushed, murmured conversations in the bedroom, so discretion was clearly of the essence.

I tried to be quiet, I really did. I carefully laid a paper baffle across the toilet pan to dampen the sound, and I tried to get things moving as gently as possible. But whatever was gurgling away in my insides had other ideas and there was a roaring like Niagara Falls as what felt like everything I'd ever eaten in my life, combined with most of my internal organs, vented themselves into the pan in a catastrophic ten second collapse.

When I re-entered the bedroom you could have cut the silence with a knife.

----- x -----

Chapter 12
The Cévennes

"Above all, do not lose your desire to walk. Every day I walk myself into a state of well-being and walk away from every illness. I have walked myself into my best thoughts, and I know of no thought so burdensome that one cannot walk away from it."
                                                                                    Søren Kierkegaard

The rain of the last few days had finally gone and I walked along chestnut terraces under a clear blue sky in a chilly wind. Occasional breaks in the trees gave me long views across the mountains.

I arrived at Saint-Germain-de-Calberte just after lunchtime, looking forward to camping in the good weather.

Saint-Germaine is a pleasant little village, set on a hillside looking out across the Cévennes. Its main attraction seems to be a bronze statue of a naked man building a pile of stones, put up as a tribute to the workers of the Cévennes. And the main attraction of the naked man statue seems to be... well, do you really need me to spell it out? It's worn shiny by the constant handling it gets, which tells you something about people and the human condition. It's a fascination which I guess has remained unchanged over millennia and I found it quite life-affirming.

My high spirits were only moderately dampened by the discovery that the only campsite was closed. I knew I was in a national park where wild camping was frowned upon; the tourist office was also closed and I still hadn't eaten, so I adjourned to a nearby park to eat lunch and consider my options.

The next campsite was too far to walk today. I could wild camp, provided I could find somewhere level enough for my tent and private enough not to be disturbed. And I'd need water. Or I could try to find a *gîte* or an *auberge* in the village. I had already passed one that looked very pleasant, although that impression may have derived from the fact that I was hot and thirsty and the inn had a shaded terrace in front of it, with locals sitting out, drinking cold beer. And if I stayed at the inn, I could get food, so when I left I'd still have a dinner and a breakfast in reserve in my rucksack.

I put my lunch rubbish in a nearby bin and re-packed my rucksack. A few minutes later, I was booked into the inn and sharing a four-berth room with a couple I'd met a few days ago. As I lay on my bed reflecting, I was very conscious that I had only 21km left to walk to St-Jean-du-Gard and then a further 26km to Ales. I was beginning to feel that I was on my way home, although I knew that the last day to Ales would be hard.

At dinner, the proprietor was keen to tell me that he had seated me with, "The other English". I was intrigued because I hadn't noticed any other English people around the inn, but when dinner came, I found I was sharing a table with three Americans: a married couple and their friend. They smiled at being mistakenly thought English and assured me that didn't happen often, although as their names were Sally, Roger and Jeff I wouldn't have been surprised if they'd told me it happened all the time. They called themselves the California Walkers.

Sally told me how her son had been looking for accommodation as a student in Los Angeles, and how he'd been interviewed by four students from England who were looking for someone suitable to take the last bed in their accommodation (and share the rent). The first question at his interview was, "What's the airspeed velocity of a swallow?"

She looked at me expectantly and I wondered if she knew the question was impossible to answer in the form she'd asked it. Before I could stop myself, I'd blurted out, "African or European?", and she started laughing.

"You would have got the room!"

My interested was piqued because they enjoyed walking and came from California, so I told Jeff of my ambition to walk the John Muir Trail through the High Sierra. This year I'd been thwarted by the permit system.

The national park authority there operates a wilderness permit system for anyone who wishes to wild camp and permits, I'd found, are difficult to obtain. An application can be made up to 24 weeks in advance, there is one telephone number for applications and that phone is staffed by one person between limited hours. Exactly 24 weeks before my intended trip, I'd spent a day and a half telephoning and listening to the engaged tone before finally getting through, only to be told that the advance permits were all gone.

Jeff's response was so simple and straightforward that I kicked myself for not thinking of it: "You should go anyway. There are plenty of places to walk in those mountains where you don't need a permit".

The California Walkers' approach to walking was one of elegant simplicity. They went to an area where they wished to walk and started walking. Distance wasn't hugely important to them and most days they covered something in the region of 10-12km. They didn't book accommodation in advance either: towards the end of each day, they'd go into a town or village and ask where they might get a room for the night. Jeff assured me that they usually ended up in an inn or someone's spare bed.

Roger and Sally were fluent in French, but the three of them had recently been to Bulgaria. None of them spoke Bulgarian, and walking through rural areas they were unlikely to encounter anyone who spoke English. I asked how they found accommodation if they couldn't make themselves understood and Jeff was relaxed: "A bit of English, a bit of miming, it's not so hard".

----- x -----

The next morning I was up early and away, walking once again through the chestnut terraces. It struck me that there must be millions upon millions of bright green chestnut leaves all around me. I'd heard it said that the Cévennes region has never known famine because of its chestnut trees. The trees provided timber, fuel, sugar, animal feed, flour for bread, soup, alcohol, coffee substitute and tannin for leather production to name just a few.

Chestnut production in the Cévennes peaked in the 18th and 19th centuries but by the 1870s, when Stevenson passed through - although unknown to him, a new type of mould was just beginning to kill the trees.

New strains were introduced by the same French scientists who'd worked to combat the phylloxera infestations that had devastated French vineyards a few years before, but as more and more people moved away from the land, chestnut production never reached its previous peak.

As I walked through Saint-Etienne-Vallee-Francaise the verges were lined with flowers, forcibly reminding me that I was missing the bluebells that would be out back home. I rounded a corner musing on the bluebell woods near my house, and the sudden smell of cut grass took me straight home to England. I paused for a swig of water and thought about home: my family, my girlfriend and my friends, and how good it would be to see them all. Better get walking then!

On a bridge spanning the river in St Etienne were two dogs, staring intently at each other across the bridge and quivering nose-to-tail from the concentration involved. It looked to me as if the slightest lapse in concentration would quickly lead to an attack, so I inched my way past, leaving them as much room as I could and disturbing them as little as possible. I looked back from farther up the hill and they were still there, posturing like mad, each refusing to blink or back down.

The way was steep up to the Col de Saint-Pierre, a mere baby at 597m, and I began picking my way down a crumbly path through pine trees. Olive trees began to appear, further developing my impression that I was at last in the south of France.

The way down to Saint-Jean-du-Gard was steep until I got to the river, then beautifully picturesque as I walked along it. I passed by two campsites, aiming for one on the other side of town to cut down the distance I would walk on my last day.

The countryside had changed markedly along the length of my walk and here it changed again. I paused to photograph a low bridge and, unusually for me, I let go of one of my trekking poles and watched dismayed as it fell onto the rocks below the bridge.

I sighed at my own cack-handedness. The nearness of my destination had kept me walking all day and, foolishly, I hadn't stopped for lunch. It was hot, I was hungry and dehydrated, and that was starting to affect my judgement and my ability.

It looked an easy climb to retrieve my pole, so I clambered down over the rocks to get to it.

Then, without warning, my left leg gave way under me and I fell in a bewildered daze, landing in a tangled heap next to my pole on the lower rocks near the river.

Surprised and somewhat shocked, and almost as if I was an uninvolved spectator, I heard myself say out loud, "What the fuck is the matter with me?", as I dragged myself into a sitting position. The shock wore off and I could feel a few bruises but no serious pain. It was the sheer somnolence of my action that upset me, so I took a few minutes to check myself over carefully and gather my wits. Clearly I needed to be much more disciplined about keeping myself fed and hydrated.

There was no real damage done so I concluded that I'd been given a cheap lesson. I took a long drink from my water bottle, picked up my pole and scrambled back up to the track.

The river path led right into the centre of Saint-Jean, which looked a lovely little town in the afternoon sun. I walked right through the town to reach the campsite I wanted: convenient for the town and on the best side of town to give me a good start when I left.

My tent was soon up and drying, with the latest lot of laundry strung from it to a nearby bush, when I noticed a man taking a very close interest in my tent. He glanced at me and moved away.

I made myself a cup of tea and relaxed, only to spot him again, this time looking me over from the other side of my pitch.

Why anyone would be interested in me I couldn't imagine, but there was one sure way to find out, so I strolled over to him with my tea and bonjoured him.

He was Jurgen, 68 years old (although you'd never believe it) and a retired surgeon from Bonn. He asked me about my tent and was fascinated that I carried everything I needed. I told him about my journey and, evidently interested, he questioned me at some length.

I was humbled when he invited me to dinner with him and his wife in their camper van. I said I'd love to come, but I had to point out that I was travelling lightweight: I had nothing I could bring. He was quite taken aback, "It is not necessary that you bring anything. We are not poor. I was a surgeon!"

He made me promise that I wouldn't bring anything, emphasising a couple of times that, "We are not poor!", but I kept my fingers crossed when I promised and as soon as he'd gone back to his camper van to fire up the barbeque, I slipped out of the campsite to try to get to the supermarket before it shut. If I couldn't contribute to the meal I could at least give his wife a box of chocolates or some flowers.

Unfortunately I'd only gone a couple of hundred metres down the road before he passed me on a bicycle, heading for the same supermarket.

He knew instantly what I was up to and he was reproachful.

"John. It is not necessary. Please don't bring anything."

This time I had to concede with good grace and I left him to cycle into town while I walked back to my tent to get cleaned up for my evening out.

----- X -----

American hikers often refer to rest days as "taking a zero", i.e. walking zero miles, and I took a zero the following day. It was quite refreshing to wander about without a rucksack on my back and I enjoyed playing the tourist for a day, seeing the sights and sending a few postcards. I bought a little food, and most importantly for my eventual journey home, some deodorant.

I wandered towards the railway station, now long-abandoned by the mainstream French railways, but still home to a tourist steam train, and as I entered the platform I was instantly reminded of my father.

The suddenness with which the memories and images came back to me was quite overwhelming. My dad had always loved steam trains and traction engines, and when I was small we'd often gone to steam fairs and traction engine rallies. Walking onto the platform had exposed me to the full whiff of a steam train, standing on the track, quietly hissing, and the smell instantaneously brought back so many memories. My dad died just five years ago and I sat down with a lump in my throat.

That night the campsite was even quieter than the last, apart from the male half of a couple from Stuttgart. He had one of those voices that cannot speak quietly and I could hear him wherever I was on the campsite. Still, I reasoned, at least he'd be quiet when he was asleep. I was able to contemplate the folly of making assumptions as I lay awake for most of the night, kept that way by his deep, resonant snoring.

The next morning I got up early for my last day of walking. After the night's performance by the man from Stuttgart I didn't feel like pussyfooting about, although sadly nothing I did in the mornings was likely to generate much noise.

I set off on my final day. I knew I had some steep paths to negotiate and I hoped to complete them in the cool of the morning. I was well fed and rested, and apart from my lunch and some water, I carried no other consumables: my pack was as light as it was ever going to be.

I made my way through quiet country lanes, eventually working downhill to a river crossing. Now the uphill started in earnest, and the navigation got more difficult, necessitating much checking and rechecking.

After a lot of sweat and effort, I reached the Col d'Uglas and turned right onto a track. From what I could see it should be mostly level walking, at height, in a straight line due east before dropping down to Ales.

My map told me that I was just 12km from Ales, at my usual pace a mere three hours walking if I took it easy. But a sign at the col told me that Ales was five and a half hours away. Clearly the next 12km must be very hard going.

That impression was quickly confirmed. I had anticipated a vehicle track for most of the way, but my path quickly turned off and narrowed. It squeezed between rocks and went up hill and down dale, across fractured limestone pavements and up and down steep dirt banks, some of the toughest terrain I'd encountered on my journey. It was hot, sweaty work and applying my learning from two days ago, I made a point of drinking water at intervals and of stopping for lunch.

Eventually I reached a hilltop and what the French call *une table d'orientation* with a couple of bench seats. I'd been travelling with my own mental vision of what Ales, my destination, would look like. I'd envisaged a golden city below me, shimmering on the plain as I regarded it from the heights like a conquering hero. Not terribly practical, maybe, but that was what was in my mind.

Now Ales lay in front of me (for that was what my map told me) and it really was a golden city, shimmering in the heat down on the plain. I can't think of an occasion when imagination and reality have so closely coincided, and that fact alone caused me to spend some time sitting in the sun and the breeze, just looking down at a view that should, I felt, have been mythical, but which actually existed right there in front of me.

Next was a long downhill stretch and the path was determined not to give up easily. I picked my way down slabby slopes, across loose rock and along narrow, rain-scoured gullies. Before long I made it to the outskirts of Ales, the metal tips of my walking poles sounding alien as they clicked on the hard road surface.

I paused for a swig of water, re-fitted the rubber tips onto my trekking poles and walked into town.

----- x -----

Every Day above a New Horizon

Appendix 1
Kit List for the Cévennes Walk

This is what I was carrying for my walk through France:

Rucksack

Tent

Sleeping bag. *(No heavier than strictly necessary – sleeping in your clothes allows you to use their insulation to supplement that of the sleeping bag and thus reduces the thickness of bag you need, and the weight of it. Why carry extra insulation – in the form of a thicker sleeping bag – that you'll only use for eight hours a day?)*

Sleeping mat. *(Important more as insulation than as padding. If you don't insulate yourself from the ground then what you're really doing is attempting to warm up the whole of Planet Earth using only your body heat. Good luck with that.)*

Water bottles/bladders

Water purifying tablets

Stove/pot

Gas cylinder

Mug

Spoon

Penknife

Map and case

Compass

Pacer beads

Head torch

Whistle

Washing / toilet kit. *(Contains: face cloth, liquid soap (for use as soap, shampoo and for washing clothes), razor, sun cream, toothbrush, miniature toothpaste, toilet kit, miniature deodorant, anti-blister dry-lubricant stick used for the prevention of, ahem, gentleman's chafing – don't use it on your feet because it will stop your wicking socks from working properly.)*

Backpacking towel. *(Weighing in at a mere 27g and about the size of a dishcloth. Use it, wring it out and then keep on using it and wringing it.)*

Emergency kit appropriate to what you're doing and where you're going. *(Mine contained: antiseptic wipes, gel blister plasters, moleskin, ibuprofen tablets, paracetamol tablets, anti-histamine tablets, anti-diarrhoea tablets, a tick remover, waterproof matches, a lighter, a back-up compass, water purifying tablets, duct tape wound round an old credit card, spare batteries for my head torch, lightweight nylon cord (doubles as washing line).)*

Camera

Sit mat

Flip-flops

Notebook and pen

Midge head net

Spare socks

Spare pants

Spare shirt

Waterproof trousers

Waterproof jacket

Fleece

Neck gaiter

Woolly hat

Sun hat

Gloves

Walking poles

Elephant

Every Day above a New Horizon

CPSIA information can be obtained
at www.ICGtesting.com
Printed in the USA
LVOW04s2312310716
498513LV00023B/524/P